I0810457

HAUNTED NORTHERN CALIFORNIA

HAUNTED NORTHERN CALIFORNIA

BRIAN CLUNE

WITH PHOTOGRAPHY BY TERRI CLUNE

Haunted America

Published by Haunted America
A division of The History Press
An imprint of Arcadia Publishing
Charleston, SC
www.historypress.com

Copyright © 2025 by Brian Clune
All rights reserved

Front cover: One cannot escape the eerie feeling Preston Castle exudes from its very bricks.

Unless otherwise noted, all photos were provided by Terri Clune.

First published 2025

Manufactured in the United States

ISBN 9781467170550

Library of Congress Control Number: 2025940391

Notice: The information in this book is true and complete to the best of our knowledge. It is offered without guarantee on the part of the author or The History Press. The author and The History Press disclaim all liability in connection with the use of this book.

All rights reserved. No part of this book may be reproduced or transmitted in any form whatsoever without prior written permission from the publisher except in the case of brief quotations embodied in critical articles and reviews.

DEDICATION

This book is dedicated to all of the folks who work tirelessly to keep the history of California alive for future generations. I also dedicate this book to my wonderful editor and friend, Laurie Krill. I would not be able to continue doing this without her support and unfailing ability to answer my questions and give advice when I ask for it—and even when I didn't but needed it anyway. I also want to dedicate this to the men and women in our armed forces, past and present. Having done more research into various aspects of our military history, I am awestruck at the dedication to duty shown by all those who serve our great nation. Once again, I need to give a dedication to the Blue Orb, who has never left my consciousness.

Most of all, I want to dedicate this book to my dear friend Scott Gruenwald. Scott was going to be my tour guide and was excited about writing the foreword for this book. Scott tragically passed away shortly before I began research for the book. I will miss you, my friend, until we meet again (please have clothes on).

The Winchester House is steeped in mystery and may be the most famous haunted house in history.

If you bury the past and forget it, there are so many things you will never know, and you will never even know you don't know.

—Cameron Brinkley, Defense Language Institute and Presidio of Monterey deputy command historian

CONTENTS

The Gingerbread B&B in Ferndale.

ACKNOWLEDGEMENTS

As I have said many times, an author cannot publish a book by themselves; it takes a team. I am lucky enough to have what I consider to be the best team on the planet here at The History Press and Arcadia Publishing. It was a rocky start for us, but I hope they know how much I appreciate every single one of the people who make me look so good as a writer. You will always have my deepest respect and gratitude. I would like to thank J'aime Rubio for her dedication to history and, even though she didn't know she was doing it, for allowing me to use some of her hard work for portions of this book. Thank you, J'aime. I also need to thank all of those who imparted their history, stories and ghostly connections. After all, what is a ghost book without the spirits? I also want to thank Ann Bender for all of the help she gave me with stories, contacts and knowledge.

The National Exchange Hotel in Nevada City is often confused for the National Hotel in Jackson. Both are quite haunted.

INTRODUCTION

We in California like to ignore our geography. We know what the boundaries are yet refuse to abide by them. We know there is no official Central Coast or Valley, and we know that Northern California begins at Sacramento. But if you try to tell folks in Monterey or San Francisco they are technically in Southern California, you may be attacked—well, verbally.

Geographical ignorance aside, Northern California is one of the most beautiful places on Earth—deep sylvan forests, pristine clear blue lakes, majestic towering mountains and towns that harken back to the time of both Mayberry and Deadwood combined to impart a feeling of tranquility mixed with history that cannot be duplicated anywhere else. However, this beauty hides a past of violence, human suffering, disaster and death that remains in the spirits of all the ethnicities who lived and died in the region make haunted Northern California what it is today.

NEVADA CITY AND GRASS VALLEY

Nevada City? In a book about California? What the hell am I thinking? Well, I am thinking about a city that was named long before the neighboring state of Nevada became a state and afterward had to add the word "city" to its name to avoid confusion about its actual location.

Nevada City and its sister city of Grass Valley, located about five miles away, sprang up during the gold rush era in lands that historically belong to the Nisenan tribe. According to the Nisenan people, they have been wrongly lumped in with the Maidu, Southern Maidu and "digger" peoples; the Nisenan are a separate tribe with their own "cultural lifeways." Their towns were places with extended family groups, each led by a *huk* (headsman) or *mayan* (headwoman), with their own distinct geographic area and language. The Nisenan lived in relative peace, that is until the California Gold Rush began causing the people some problems.

Already having their numbers depleted by a severe malaria epidemic in the 1830s, in which an estimated 75 percent of the Nisenan population died, after gold was discovered in California, hundreds of thousands of people joined the fur trappers who were already invading the Nisenan peoples' territory. In only a few years' time, the miners had appropriated large areas of Nisenan land and brought new diseases and more violence to the area. The Nisenan people left the immediate area to settle deeper into their traditional lands.

With much of the Nisenan land taken, Chief Charlie Cully negotiated a land deal with President Woodrow Wilson in 1913. That land, which was obtained in 1887, would become federal trust land and thereby protected from further theft. Wilson agreed, and the Nevada City Rancheria was established and the tribal government was federally recognized. Unfortunately, in the 1950s and '60s, the California state government passed the California Rancheria Termination Act, which illegally bypassed federal law in favor of state law. The Nisenan tribe and their supporters have been fighting the state bureaucracy ever since, and most of the rancherias have been restored. But the Nisenan people are still waiting for federal recognition and are still fighting to regain their stolen land.

Nevada City, like many other towns in Gold Country, sprang up after gold was discovered by John Sutter's employee James Marshall while working at Sutter's Mill in 1848. First known as Deer Creek Dry Diggins, the settlement began along Deer Creek but later became known as Caldwell's Upper Store after Dr. A.B. Caldwell opened a store four miles upriver from one he already owned. Neither of these names were official, and folks who came into the area knew the settlement by one or the other depending on where they came from. With so many folks coming to hunt for their fortunes, businesses sprang up, with the first "broad" building being erected by Madame Penn in the spring of 1850. The first hotel in town, the Nevada Hotel, was built in April the same year, and then the flood of families began to pour in and Caldwell's Upper Store grew like a weed.

On April 16, 1850, while the local vote for city magistrate was being counted, a crowd assembled outside of one of the hotels. Reports of the crowd size varied widely, saying between 30 and 250 waited for the results of the election. After the winner was announced, someone suggested the town needed a name, a "real name." Right then and there, slips of paper were passed out, and folks wrote down their suggestions. It is still unclear just how the name came about, but in 1856, district attorney, future senator and newspaper editor Aaron Sargent wrote, "As the mountains were 'snowy,' and the winter had been a 'snowy' one, it was not a strange idea of calling the place 'snowy,' 'snow covered' or 'nevada' as the word is in Spanish." It is said that the name was first suggested by store owner Octavius Blackman, but his partner, Edward Truex, claimed that it was he who thought of the name first. Whichever is true, from April 1850, the name of the town was forever Nevada City.

There is a myth that says Nevada City was forced to change its name from Nevada to Nevada City due to its neighboring state assuming that name when it became a state in 1861. The truth of the matter is far different. As noted, Nevada City had its name eleven years before Nevada officially entered the United States as the Nevada Territory (it didn't become a state until 1864, fourteen years later). From 1850 through the 1860s, Nevada City was referred to as the City of Nevada, the Township of Nevada or, as usually happened, simply Nevada. The state itself had originally decided on the name Sierra Nevada but shortened it to Nevada later. So, for folks who think Nevada City stole the name, it was actually the other way around.

As was the case with many mining towns and Old West structures, fire was something that could be a danger for wooden buildings. Now, toss in the incredible pine forest Nevada City was built among, and you have a recipe for disaster. The first—and some say the worst—fire in the city's history occurred at two o'clock in the morning on March 11, 1851. It is said that it was "undoubtedly the work of incendiarism. Three men were denounced as incendiaries by committee of inquiry of the citizens, and would have been instantly hung, had they been taken." Once the pine trees ignited and their burning sap fell onto dry roofs, timber and the like, it didn't take long for much of the town to become engulfed. By the time the fire was extinguished, 175 structures had been destroyed. Homes, saloons, hotels and shops were simply gone. The miners and their families were not deterred, however, and when they did rebuild, they began using brick and other fire-resistant material. They even added six inches of sand between the ceilings and roofs of some buildings in the hopes that if the structure began to burn, the sand would fall from the top and put out the fire inside.

Over the years, Nevada City has produced many firsts and can claim some big names in our nation's history as part of their own history, including three U.S. senators, William Stewart, George Hearst and A.A. Sargent, who all lived in Nevada City, along with President Herbert Hoover, who lived and worked in Nevada City during his gold mining days. When several water companies merged into the Pacific Gas and Electric Company (PG&E), their first office was located in Nevada City, and the town can also boast numerous inventions that helped revolutionize mining, water and electrical systems around the country and the world.

Today, Nevada City is a tourist town where folks come to get a small glimpse of what life was like in the days when gold ruled the hills and life was both simpler and more complex. Thanks to two people in the area, David Osborne and Charles Woods, the town was saved from decay with the adoption of city ordinance #338 in 1968. Thanks to these men, as well as the citizens of Nevada City, we have a beautiful and historic location to visit and, for the paratraveler, to hunt ghosts in a truly charming, very haunted location.

The Broad Street Inn is known for its comfort and friendly spirits.

Like many California gold rush towns, Nevada City had a tumultuous growth; miners fighting over claims, drunken bar fights and long, painful diseases claimed many lives. This type of human suffering can and will cause spirits to remain in places where they felt comfortable or in areas where they needed to get justice. Nevada City is no different. Many think that ghosts are scary, frightening or dark, but many—even most—are nothing of the sort. One location in Nevada City has spirits that are not scary in the least; in fact, they are downright welcoming.

The Broad Street Inn is a bed-and-breakfast within walking distance of the historic downtown area of Nevada City. I was drawn to the charming home and decided to take a few pictures when I saw the owners busy with the upkeep. When I asked if they had any spirits, they hesitated in telling me "Yes, but they aren't scary." So, they were unsure if I wanted to mention them, but of course I did! They told me that the spirits who occupied their inn were all past family members of those who'd owned the home, and they not only greet new guests with kind, whispered "hellos," but they have also, in the past, warned the owners of things that needed repair. The current owners said that they and their guests have seen a kindly woman sitting at a window, looking out at the world, who will give a smile and nod to guests and folks walking past before going back to her musings. The spirits will also, on occasion, join guests for breakfast, and they will accompany the owners, who live on-site, for other meals. The spirits, owners and guests all feel welcome and at ease with the kindly, otherworldly caretakers. So, if you need a place to stay while in Nevada City, please consider the Broad Street Inn as your home away from home.

McGee's Pub, located on Broad Street in the center of town, is your typical small-town watering hole—but with a seemingly dark past. I was told by one of the bartenders and one of the patrons that there once was an old jail cell in the basement that had housed Chinese prisoners. This was due to the racism at the time toward the Chinese and the desire to keep them separated from other criminals. I was told that strange things happen down in this area, especially feelings of being watched and employees' skin crawling while gathering supplies to bring up to the bar. Many of the staff have heard their names being whispered while in the basement, and others have heard whispered Chinese coming from the shadowed corners of the darkened space. I was told that many of the bar's employees refuse to go into the basement alone due to not only hearing strange sounds but also from seeing movement out of the corner of their eyes that cannot be explained. I was allowed access to this basement area, and what I can tell you is that the atmosphere in the cramped space is, shall we say, different.

While in another bar, asking about their ghosts (unfortunately, they weren't talking), I ran into the former owner of the once Union Hotel. The building is no longer a hotel, but it is now a restaurant on the ground floor called The Speakeasy, while the upper floor was converted into office space. The old owner told me that the hotel was so haunted that it was unusual to not hear from guests after a night's stay. At the hotel, guests would complain about kids running up and down the hall all night long, making noise, laughing and, well, just being kids. The odd thing about this is that it would happen when no kids were staying at the hotel. The phones in the rooms would call the front desk at all hours, but no one would be on the other end. And housekeeping would find rooms in a shambles when no one had spent the night in the room. These things happened so often that housekeeping was told to check each room daily while making their rounds. A gentleman who was sitting with the old owner mentioned that he had gone up after the sale while helping the owner move out and had heard all sorts of noises and what sounded like items being moved around, but he couldn't find anyone. He was alone in the hotel. The former owner also said that the ground floor of the old Union Hotel was almost as haunted as the upper floor and that The Speakeasy's Communal Café must be pretty haunted as well. Unfortunately, the staff at the restaurant wouldn't speak to me about any haunting activity, yet a few of the customers grinned at me while nodding in agreement that it surely occurred.

No paranormal chapter about Nevada City would be complete without writing about the National Exchange Hotel. Often confused with the National Hotel that once stood in the same city and the other National Hotel in Jackson, California, the National Exchange in Nevada City is just as historic as the other two and, at the very least, as haunted as its counterpart in Jackson. The hotel itself is trying to move away from its haunted past and reputation, and its employees wouldn't talk to me about their haunts. However, luckily, I ran into a former employee who was more than willing to speak of the ghosts that haunt the historic inn. This former employee said that there are quite a few rooms that are very active and claimed they had a lot of experiences there while working and staying at the National Exchange Hotel.

According to the employee, rooms 208 and 319 may be the two most haunted rooms; however, when this person stayed in room 209, which had mysteriously been completely boarded up before the hotel renovated it, the entire night was fraught with the feeling that they were being watched. And when the power went out due to a raging snowstorm, the feeling rose to the point of being almost unbearable. A while later, while the employee was working the front desk, a guest told them that on a previous visit, they had stayed in room 209 and taken a short video to show her mother where she was staying. After sending the video, her mother called back and asked what was wrong. She went on to tell her daughter that there was something odd about the video and asked if her phone was OK. When the guest went back and looked at the video, she saw what her mother was talking about. In the middle of the video, the shot goes into slow motion, but then a "horrible screeching is heard, followed by dark terrible noises." The odd thing about the noises is that they are not in slow motion. The employee went on to say that a month later, another guest, while staying in the same room, told the employee that the same thing happened to them "last night."

In an episode of *Ghost Adventures*, the crew investigated room 402, where a standoff with police ended with a man killing himself. I won't go into the episode, but I was told that the hotel manager once stayed in that room with her dog. After only a short time, the manager's dog began to bark at something unseen in the room, and no matter what the manager did, the dog just wouldn't stop barking at the seemingly empty air. The manager was finally forced to move into another room, where the dog promptly settled

The "basement" of McGee's Pub was once a jail cell for Chinese prisoners.

down and went to sleep. Also on the fourth floor, room 411 seems to have a spirit that has an affinity for her picture. If the picture was moved, the spirit would become angry and cause quite a bit of mischief. She also seems to be able to use the energy around her to put up a force field, for lack of a better word. One guest had trouble getting into this room after the picture fell under the bed. He opened the door, but according to the guest, he was unable to go through the doorway due to some sort of weird "energy field." Once hotel staff arrived, they were all able to enter the room and it was then they noticed the picture partially under the bed. Once the picture was back in its proper place, the guest had no more trouble getting into the room. The picture has now been permanently removed from the room.

The employee told me that while working in room 309, they heard the door of room 308 being unlocked; they then watched as the lock turned and the door slowly opened. Thinking that the air-conditioning might have been left on or a window left open, the employee checked the room but found nothing open or left on. This is the room where it is said a woman was murdered. A couple on their honeymoon stayed in 208 on their wedding night, but they asked if they could change rooms because the lights kept turning off and on and the TV did the same. "Ghost calls" come in from what sounds like kids who say they are staying in room numbers from past eras. They say they are scared because there are men in the room next door. Supposedly, there was a brothel in the hotel with soiled doves who had their kids living with them; many believe these phantom calls may be from these lost children. There have been a few reports of a little girl singing on a different floor of the hotel; she could be one of the kids making the "ghost calls."

Nevada City certainly has an abundance of spirit activity within its boundaries, and every paratraveler will find a veritable paranormal playground to explore here. Of course, Nevada City is not alone. Grass Valley, Nevada City's sister city, is only five miles away, and we cannot forget to visit if one wants to have a tasty Cornish pasty and find even more spirits and places to explore.

GRASS VALLEY

Grass Valley, like Nevada City, was originally part of the Nisenan tribe's land, and just like its sister city, Grass Valley acquired land from the tribe. It is said that in the late 1840s, a group of cattlemen made notations about the area and stated that, "while searching for a place to graze, we came upon a grassy valley." This is what led to the eventual naming of the city. Like so many other cities and towns in California Gold Country, Grass Valley grew rapidly after quartz gold was discovered, with mines opening up everywhere in the area. Grass Valley mines made the city the richest in California mining history. Due to the plethora of mines springing up, men were needed to toil for the gold. These miners came from all over the globe, and the best were Cornish.

The legend of the Cornish miners goes back before the West was even "tamed," having come to the American East Coast to seek work around 1815. Their prowess in the art of mining was unmatched. Bringing a strong work ethic and innovation to the trade, Cornish miners were so sought after that mine owners up and down the East Coast would ask those who were already working for them if they knew anyone back home who might need a job and be willing to come to America. Many of the Cornish would say, "Well, I know a *Cousin Jack* that might be interested." There is some debate about where the term *Cousin Jack* originated, but history is clear that a Cousin Jack was a nickname for a Cornish miner. It is said that by the 1890s, a full 60 percent of the population of Grass Valley was Cornish. Even today, the Cornish influence on the town is prominent. It is

The Book Seller in Grass Valley's historic downtown has its own ghost reader.

one of the only places in California where one can buy an original Cornish meat pie known as a pasty.

By the end of World War II, with the mines shutting down, a steady decline came about, and the last major mining operation ended in the mid-1950s. As the 1960s began, Grass Valley was fading, but as with Nevada City, a new arrival stepped in to open a business in the town. Almost overnight, the town's fortunes seemed to brighten. In 1979, the downtown merchants established the Grass Valley Downtown Association, and in 1986, the group began using the National Trust for Historic Preservation's Main Street Program. Today, Grass Valley has been brought back to life as a tourist destination, and combined with Nevada City, it holds joint parades and events that draw folks from all over Gold Country and beyond. With Cornish restaurants serving tasty pasties and the revitalized downtown shopping scene, those living in Grass Valley, as well as those spirits that remain, are proud to call Grass Valley home.

Like with Nevada City, no paranormal chapter about Grass Valley would be complete without the Holbrooke Hotel being mentioned. Both the Holbrooke and the National Exchange Hotel have the same owner, and as such, getting them to open up about their resident spirits was not possible. And I was not lucky enough to run into a former employee like I did with the National Exchange Hotel. However, the Holbrooke is famous enough for its ghosts that many stories exist. In fact, with so many famous past guests, such as Presidents Ulysses S. Grant, Benjamin Harrison and James Garfield, the Holbrooke may be—or should be—even more famous than the Nevada Exchange. Its other distinguished guests include authors Bret Harte and Samuel Clemens, along with prize fighter "Gentleman Jim" Corbett and Bob Fitzsimmons. It is even rumored that notorious bandit Black Bart stayed at the Holbrooke between robberies. One can see why the hotel is a draw for folks to remain here after death.

According to several travel sites, the Holbrooke may be the most haunted hotel in Northern California. One of the ghosts that is seen most is a chambermaid named Sarah, who fell to her death from the hotel and can be seen near the stairs of the Holbrooke. Local historian Mark Lyon, who goes by the nickname "Ghost Man," has been investigating the Holbrooke for many years and also gives haunted tours of Grass Valley. Lyon has appeared on the hit show *My Ghost Story*, talking about the ghosts of the Holbrooke, and he has mentioned that several children can be heard playing in the hallways of the hotel and will even be heard "jumping" on old spring mattresses that no longer exist. He talked about how folks who stay in room 9 often wake up to the previously mentioned chambermaid folding the clothes they have left out. He also talked about how a frightening vision of a distraught gambler, who died by suicide after slitting his own throat, has been seen in a room, lying in a pool of blood with the razorblade still at his side. There is proof of this death by suicide in the form of a letter that can be found at the Doris Foley Library in Nevada City. Lyon also has a photo, taken by a couple who stayed at the Holbrooke, which seems to show the most famous ghost of the hotel, a menacing cowboy in Victorian clothes wearing a cowboy hat.

It seems obvious that the Holbrooke, just like the National Exchange, is a place that every paratraveler should put on their travel list. This is not the only location in Grass Valley that has its share of spirit activity, however.

The Del Oro Theater, just down the street from the Holbrooke, is known for showing first-run movies and for its ghosts showing themselves. This Art Deco masterpiece, built in 1941–42, has several known and unknown ghosts haunting its theaters (it is now a triplex). *Los Angeles* magazine (October 1, 2024) said that guests have reported apparitions brushing up against them while watching movies, as if they are heading for empty seats. The article also claimed that a "woman in white" (there always seems to be a woman in white in my books), who was reportedly pushed from the theater's fire escape, is often seen. Employees say that even though there are many stories of ghosts haunting the Del Oro, this is the one that creeps them out the most. As seems to be the case with most movie theaters, there is a story about a phantom projectionist who haunts the projection room. In this case, he was supposedly burned to death in a freak fire.

Another story from *Los Angeles* magazine says that folks have seen "creepy twins" playing in the hallways of the theater, and it's said that these twins could give the girls from *The Shining* a run for their money. Mark Lyon seems to be able to confirm the twins' existence, if not the creepiness of their nature. Lyon told the Automobile Club of America (September 5, 2023) that during one of his haunted walking tours of Grass Valley, his group was standing outside the theater by the ticketing booth when popcorn began raining down on them from the roof of the building. A few days later, during another tour and while standing in the same spot, confetti, in the form of torn-up concession napkins, began falling on their heads. He said that two members of his tour group could clearly see a little girl standing at the edge of the roof, laughing as she tossed the bits of paper down on the group. It was later confirmed by the theater's management that the door to the roof had been securely locked.

Another location that gets a hauntable mention, a small bookstore called the Book Seller, is located right between the Holbrooke Hotel and Del Oro Theater. The clerks told me that they have to keep putting books back on the shelves due to them constantly "falling" to the floor. They said they can never find a reason for this and that it happens often enough that they know there is something going on that is not "normal." They often feel a strange vibration in the floor, but it is nowhere near strong enough to cause the books to fall, and there is no reason—nor can they find any explanation—for the vibration. They also told me that the bookstore's printer will randomly print a smiley face. They never know when this will occur, but there are times that they will turn the printer on and find there is already a paper in the tray with a smiley face or two printed on it, even though the tray should have been shut. The manager of the Book Seller also told me that when she was manager of the Lazy Dog Chocolatier, a couple of doors down from the bookstore, there were always odd things happening there. She told me that once, while coming up from the basement of the chocolate shop, she heard glass shattering from below. As she went back down to investigate what had broken, she found that the florescent bulbs that are normally stored in a "fool-proof" rack had all mysteriously fallen and shattered on the basement floor. Another time, while in the same basement, she dropped something and heard the sound of muffled male laughter. She knew that you could hear customers in the

The Holbrooke Hotel, like its cousin in Nevada City, shies away from its ghosts.

shop above, so when she came back up, she asked who the man was who had been laughing. She was told that the only folks who had come into the chocolate shop were a woman and her daughter. The only two working at that time were the manager and another female clerk. Unfortunately, the Lazy Dog Chocolatier was not interested in talking with me.

Nevada City and Grass Valley are in one of the most beautiful spots of California. Close to the Sierra, Lake Tahoe and nestled in a pristine pine forest, this Gold Country paradise should not be missed by paratravelers, as there are so many haunted locations in the area that one can spend weeks exploring. But there are not only paranormal sites but also beautiful scenery. And don't forget, while staying in either town, trying an authentic Cornish pasty is a must.

OLD SACRAMENTO

The name Sacramento has become synonymous with California. Being the state capital of California, Sacramento has been all over the national news. The state has been both lambasted and praised for its politics, environmental stances and the way in which it treats its citizens. The sad part about everything the city *is* known for is that it overshadows the things it *should* be known for: the beauty that surrounds the city; the history that shaped not only the state but, in many cases, also the rest of the United States; the allure of the shimmering river from which the city gets its name; and, of course, the California Gold Rush, which brought thousands of folks from around the world to settle in this growing city. Sacramento was not always the capital, but once it was established, there was no stopping it. Through floods, fire, earthquakes, riots and other adversity, the city has grown to become one of the most well-known capitals in the country. It has become a center for trade and tourism and is a resource unmatched for those looking to explore the diverse cultural, economic and tourism history of the State of California. Did I mention that Sacramento is one of the most haunted cities in California—and possibly the country?

The original inhabitants of the area we know as Sacramento were the Nisenan (Southern Maidu) people. Along with the Modoc and Miwok, the tribe spread out into what is now Gold Country, hunting, fishing, farming and trapping over a wide area of Northern California. In 1808, when Spanish explorer Gabriel Moraga came across two beautiful rivers in the north-central area of Alta (upper) California, he named one Rio de las

Calaveras, or River of Skulls. The name was related to the large number of skulls found along the riverbanks. Moraga believed that these skulls came from the people who lived here who had been killed, either in tribal battle or because of famine. Moraga gave the other river a much more peaceful and serene name, Rio de los Sacramentos. When Moraga and his party came into the Sacramento Valley, the beauty of the area took their breath away. One of the expedition members wrote, "Canopies of oaks and cottonwoods… overhung both sides of the blue current. Birds chattered in the trees and fish darted through the pellucid depths. The air was like champagne and we drank deep of it. Drank in the beauty around them. It is like the Blessed Sacrament." Moraga must have agreed.

Once Mexico gained control of Alta California, it all but ignored the northern reaches, that is until 1839, when Mexico City granted Swiss citizen John Sutter (he was actually born in Baden, Germany, but was a Swiss citizen) a large land grant of fifty thousand acres. By 1840, Sutter had established Nueva Helvetia (New Switzerland) and built Sutter's Fort. Sutter's Fort was basically a fortified trading post with high adobe walls and a gate in the middle that surrounded various shops, such as a those of a carpenter and gunsmith, a bakery and a general store. Sutter had created a place where folks could settle down, set up farms and ranches, build homesteads and grow the area into a community. Then in 1848, Sutter's chief carpenter, James Marshall, discovered a shiny piece of metal in the water next to the sawmill he was building at Sutter's Mill, and the rush was on—the California Gold Rush, that is. Thousands of folks from around the world came to stake their claims and make their fortunes. The area was changed forever and grew like a weed at the expense of John Sutter's own fortunes.

Sutter had always been a generous man, and his son John A. Sutter Jr. tried everything he could to make his father realize that with the debts he had accumulated, coupled with his generous nature, the family was going broke. Against his father's wishes, Sutter Jr. and his partner had already laid out the new city of Sacramento a few miles south of Sutter's Fort. Even though Sutter and Marshall had tried to keep the discovery of gold a secret, thousands of people from around the world descended on the area and began squatting on Sutter's land, stealing his property and taking the gold that was rightfully his, as it had been found on his land. Once the new American government in Washington, D.C., denied Sutter's Mexican land grant, his ruination was complete. Sutter deeded what land he had left to his son, who made it a part of the new city. As the City of Sacramento began profiting from the mining trade, it grew rapidly, and as more people moved

Visiting Old Sacramento is like traveling back in time.

in, the city's coffers and revenue grew as well. By 1854, the city had just over ten thousand residents, and it was chosen as the new state capital.

Since the city was set at the confluence of the Sacramento and American Rivers, it was not uncommon for it to experience floods during heavy rain and snowmelt. It was just one of those things that folks put up with. However, in 1850, the first in a series of devastating floods occurred. Homes were destroyed, crops were ruined and livestock was drowned. To make sure that nothing like this happened again, the first levee in Sacramento was built in 1852. A month after its completion, the first major storm of the season hit. The new levee failed, and Sacramento flooded once again. A new levee was, for a second time, erected, but this one also broke and, once more, the city flooded. Then on November 2, 1852, a fire broke out and burned down more than 80 percent of the city. This fire became known as the "Great Conflagration." Even with all of the disasters and a deadly cholera epidemic, which broke out in 1850, Sacramento's nearness to the gold fields kept the city growing.

Sacramento became the western terminus of the Pony Express, started the first railroad in California and had its own steamer service along the river. And four of Sacramento's businessmen, Leland Stanford, Charles Crocker, Mark Hopkins and Collis Huntington, financed the Central Pacific

Railroad, which, along with the Union Pacific Railroad, completed the first transcontinental railroad in the United States when they met in 1869 at Promontory Point in Utah. Sacramento was surely growing and becoming what many would call a "metropolitan" area, but its residents knew that there was still a chance of a devastating flood that could drown all of their hopes. Then from December 1861 to January 1862, the worst flooding in Sacramento history occurred. This flood became known as the Great Flood of 1862. The powers that be finally decided that something permanent had to be done.

So catastrophic was the Great Flood that newly elected Governor Leland Stanford had to travel to his own inauguration in a rowboat. The city was in ruins, and the citizens were up in arms. They demanded an end to the constant flooding; since the levees didn't work, the government had to find another solution. The only thing they could think of doing was raising the city itself. This massive undertaking began in 1862 with the erection of reinforced brick walls, and then the spaces were filled with millions of tons of compacted dirt. Once the new foundations were set, many of what used to be the ground floors of many of the buildings became their basements, and what used to be sidewalks were either buried or simply left where they were, leaving open spaces between some buildings and the old street. In this way, the entire city of Sacramento (at that time) was raised above the flood zone; the entire project was completed by the mid-1870s. In the years that followed, quite a few of these "open" spaces were either filled in or simply destroyed by ongoing development. However, due to the efforts of historians, it is still possible to see the remnants of what has become known as the "Sacramento Underground" by taking a tour provided by the Sacramento History Museum in Old Town Sacramento.

One advantage of the city growing along the Sacramento River was that taxes could be levied by the city on goods that were unloaded at the docks and then loaded onto the railcars. Sacramento had one of the largest railyards in the West. These railroads delivered goods to the towns and camps in Gold Country and beyond and became a welcome source of income for the fast-growing city. This revenue grew after the river was dredged in 1899 and then again in 1913. This dredging allowed seasonal access to the Pacific, increasing what goods could be shipped solely by river travel. Then in 1963, a new canal was opened into San Francisco Bay, making it possible for year-round travel to a deepwater port. This greatly increased the amount of goods that were shipped into Sacramento for distribution to inland locations.

Tower Bridge is the shortest state highway in California.

As more and more people and their automobiles came to live in the Sacramento area, it became necessary to build new roads. As the twentieth century dawned, boats, along with both freight and passenger trains, were the most common modes of traveling into and out of Sacramento. Traveling by horse and buggy, as well as walking, was how folks got around the city itself; cars were not even a thought in most people's minds. However, by the 1930s, automobiles were on the rise. By 1934, automobile traffic had increased by 700 percent, and it became obvious that the two-lane bridge that spanned the Sacramento River had become obsolete. To solve this problem, a vertical lift Art Deco–style bridge was erected. This design allowed for a wider area of transit, and since the entire span could be raised and lowered at the rate of one foot per second, delays were cut substantially. Opened on December 15, 1935 (completed in record time), the Tower Bridge is still in operation to this day. This bridge has the distinction of being the shortest state highway in California, as it spans a mere 738 feet in total.

Sacramento, like so many other cities in California, took part in one of the most reprehensible and unconstitutional acts in the history of the United States. After the bombing of Pearl Harbor, which brought the United States into World War II, and with tensions and racism running high, President Franklin D. Roosevelt signed Executive Order 9066. This order directed that all persons of Japanese descent along the West Coast were to be rounded up and "evacuated" to "relocation" camps, by force if necessary. There was no distinction made between American citizens, naturalized citizens or those legally living in the country with a visa. The order was carried out with fervor, and those rounded up in the Sacramento area were taken from their homes and temporarily housed in the Walerga (Sacramento Assembly Center), which was hastily put into operation after the order was signed. This center was placed at the location of a former migrant labor camp.

The "inmates" began arriving on May 13, 1942, with the first 600 of roughly 3,800 Japanese Americans walking through the gates of their temporary home. The camp's population peaked at 4,739, almost all of whom were from Sacramento. After a relatively short stay at Walerga, the Japanese internees were sent on to Tule Lake Internment Camp. This camp was the largest of the ten War Relocation Authority camps and would also become the most conflict-ridden camp in the system. When Roosevelt issued his Executive Order, it became the largest unconstitutional order in the history of the United States, and it remains so to this day. By a single signature, the due process rights of 120,000 American citizens were violated when they were illegally imprisoned. Tule Lake was the last camp to close

The Art Deco design of the Tower Bridge is hard to miss.

after the war. Tule Lake was in operation the longest of all the relocation camps. Walerga had the shortest operational life of any of the processing centers, as it was in operation for only fifty-two days. Let us hope that we always remember what happened so that we never allow it to occur again.

Sacramento has seen so many changes over the years that it is hard to pinpoint any one as its main diverging point, yet each one has contributed to what the city is today. From the many cultures who came to live in Sacramento, the ones who set up their businesses and those that have made the delta a hub of commerce and activity, Sacramento is the whole of all of these parts. One thing that many may not think about regarding the city's character are the people who helped shape the capital of California and who remain to this day, long after their deaths, in a quest to keep the history alive for those who seek this knowledge. The ghosts of old Sacramento are not simply a part of Old Town Sacramento; they are, in fact, the heart of the old city, which beats for those paratravelers who are brave enough to listen.

The Eagle Theater is a reconstruction of the original playhouse that, after only three months in operation, was destroyed in the great Sacramento flood of 1850. The original building was made simply of a wooden frame, with canvas walls and a tin roof. The reconstruction was built to last much longer. The Eagle Theater was the first building erected in California to specifically be used as a theater. After the theater was rebuilt, facing a different direction and with a different name, the Tehama Theater, it had a long career entertaining those in and around Sacramento's waterfront. For sixty years, the Tehama stayed open, even as the waterfront diminished into Sacramento's "skid row" but would eventually disappear from memory.

Finally, after more than one hundred years, the area was slated for redevelopment into what is now Old Sacramento. By 1970, Old Sacramento was becoming more popular, and efforts were underway to repair and reconstruct the old buildings, including the old Eagle/Tehama Theater. After more than two years of researching done by the Junior League, fundraising and obtaining government appropriations, construction began, and the new Eagle Theater opened its doors on March 14, 1974, with, appropriately enough, an 1845 comedy called *Fashion*. Today, the Eagle Theater is operated by the California State Railroad Museum and functions as a community theater and event venue. It also holds other Old Sacramento events. Folks come to enjoy the theater, and it seems that there are plenty of spirits that like the Eagle Playhouse as well.

Many people believe that the Eagle Theater is haunted by a director from the 1970s. No one knows who he is, only that he likes to make himself known by taking folks' belongings from various areas in the theater and placing them downstairs in the greenroom. The items can only be found after the show is over, never before. If, after a show, there are any chairs left onstage overnight, those chairs will be moved around from the spots where they were left. Many of the actors and musicians have talked about hearing voices while onstage, distracting them from their lines or song lyrics, and it is not unusual to have severe cold spots come up unexpectedly. Disembodied footsteps are often heard during shows, while crews are working or cleaning and even when tours of the theater are being given. One report even said that an "eerie laugh" was heard, as if a patron was enjoying a show. The theater was empty aside from the person who gave the report.

A story I found on Reddit said that while an employee was working one evening, cleaning after a show, they placed a bag of trash on the top of the stairs (the stairs led to the basement, which is actually the original ground floor) and went back to cleaning. A few minutes later, a coworker came up and asked why the bag of trash had been put at the bottom of the stairs, because the trash bins were outside on the ground level. Confused, the person went to look, and sure enough, the trash was now at the bottom (there is a turn halfway down the stairs), neatly placed and upright in the middle of the floor in front of the stairs. A little while later, this same employee was alone in the theater, putting the cleaning equipment away in the basement, when they suddenly found themselves in the dark. Panicked, they hurried to the light switch and found it had been turned off. Then they quickly left the building.

Even though the Eagle Theater of today is a modern reproduction of the original sitting on the old foundation, the ghosts of the theater don't seem to know the difference—or simply don't care. Either way, that is a good thing for us paratravelers.

As we have seen, after the flood of 1862, Old Sacramento was raised, and the ground floors of many of the buildings became their basements. This area has become known as the Sacramento Underground. There is a lot of confusion about what the underground is, with some folks describing it as a vast underground city that was once Sacramento and others likening it to the Portland, Oregon underground. The reality is a letdown for most folks, as the underground in Sacramento, at least those areas that are accessible, simply comprises two relatively small areas situated under a couple of buildings. There are a few other areas that were once part of the underground, but one now houses a miniature golf course and the other has become a pizza restaurant. There are a couple of interesting tales about ghosts, however. While talking with one of the tour guides, he told me that even though he is not a believer in ghosts, something happened during a tour that he couldn't understand. He said that he and his group were in a section of the underground when a guest asked if it was haunted. The tour guide said he didn't believe in ghosts, and then the entire group heard a very strange noise that neither he nor anyone else could explain. He said the guests were still laughing about it as they moved to another section, and then, when they stopped again, the subject was brought up once more. Before the guide could answer, they heard the noise again, followed by a short chuckle that had not come from any of the group's members. He told me that he is not ready to call it paranormal but can't explain what happened either.

The story from the tour guide is nothing compared to what other folks have reported in the basements (underground) of the two buildings the tour explores. Many guests have had the feeling that an unseen specter is following close behind or by their side as they walk through the underground; they have also heard phantom knocks, footsteps and disembodied voices. Folks have pointed out extreme cold spots in the basement areas, which seem to form just before strange shadows or, on rare occasions, full-bodied apparitions appear. There are also reports of a black-hatted cowboy, which many believe will let out spine-tingling laughter and then start yelling at the tour guests from the darkness. Even though the size and scope of the underground has been exaggerated over the years, the possibility of a paranormal encounter should convince anyone to tour the basement depths of the Sacramento Underground. Tours of the underground are led by costumed docents from the Sacramento History Museum.

The Sacramento History Museum may lead the possibly haunted underground tour, but it also may have a ghost of its own. The spirit is thought to be that of a young, twelve-year-old girl. The museum, like the Eagle Theater, is not housed in the original building that once stood there; it is, in fact, a replica. The original was a waterworks building, officers' quarters, a jail and sheriff's office, a library and a city hall. During the building's iteration as a jail, criminals were often tried, sentenced and hanged within the building, sometimes within an hour of conviction. And it is known that at least one hanging took place on a beam in the original building that was reused during the reconstruction of the museum. Many believe that some of the strange happenings in the museum may be from the victim of this hanging. There is another possibility, however.

May Hollister Woolsey was a typical young, twelve-year-old girl. She loved to write, draw and play with dolls and her friends. Unfortunately, being that it was 1879, medicine was still what we would now consider primitive, and there is some confusion on what her actual cause of death might have been. The accepted theory is that May died from encephalitis on September 21, 1879. Whatever the true cause of her death, her mother and father were devastated, and May being their only child made matters worse. Being the Victorian era, with spiritualism on the rise, May's mother sought out a medium, who charged to make contact with her daughter. We don't know the true answer to the question, but what we do know is that May's parents packed all of their daughter's belongings into a trunk and put it away. The story might have ended here, however, one hundred years later, in 1979, the current owner of the house discovered May's trunk concealed in the home, and a mystery was born.

In the trunk were items that one would expect to find among a young girl's belongings: dolls, marbles, sewing items and the like. But what stood out was a letter, seemingly written by May to her mother after her death. The letter read,

> *Dear Mama*
>
> *I am so happy as I did write you and say I was happy. Now mama dear, do not weep for me. I am not dead, only gone before to wait your coming when you will be out of all sorrow and care and will be happy with me. Oh, what pleasure there is in the spirit life no one can tell. Only think of everlasting life and pleasure where we know no sorrow; all is sunshine, there is no cloud to darken our path as on earth; we have our choice of mission.*

Many believe that this letter never actually existed, and others say that the medium wrote the letter while channeling May. Still others claim that the medium faked the whole thing as a way of scamming the grieving mother out of more money. Whatever the case may be, the letter was found in the trunk, giving the impression the mother believed it was real. There are tales of May's ghost still hanging around in the afterlife.

May Woolsey was buried in the historic Sacramento Cemetery, and folks claim that if you go to May's resting place and put your hand on her gravestone, you can feel her presence through the tingling in your hand. There are also stories of people seeing a young girl standing over the grave, with many believing it is May's spirit. Other tales say that after the trunk was opened, random screams could be heard in the home, things went missing and things were tossed around the rooms by an unseen force. It is believed that all of these strange occurrences are what caused the homeowner to give the trunk and its belongings to the Sacramento History Museum.

I was honored by the museum to be shown where May's trunk is on display, as well as another area where some of her belongings are showcased. The museum uses May's things to teach both children and adults alike what

The reconstruction of the Eagle Theatre is as haunted as the original.

life was like for a twelve-year-old in the mid- and late 1800s. I was also told that strange things have been happening in the museum ever since the trunk arrived and was put on display. Sounds of a little girl's laugh are heard when there are no children present, things are moved after the museum closes and staff leave for the evening and disembodied footsteps and taps are felt on museum guests' shoulders in a playful game of tag, to name a few. There is nothing ever scary or dangerous that occurs, only the signs of a child enjoying her afterlife at the museum.

One other place in Old Sacramento that must be mentioned is Evangeline's Costume Store. With more than just costumes, Evangeline's is like the old Spencer's gift store, Hot Topic and a Spirit Halloween store all rolled up into one, and the best thing about it are the actual ghosts. One of the managers was kind enough to show me around, tell me some tales and mentioned that the basement had some strange activity. I was told that employees will see a man in a top hat, sometimes wearing fishing attire and boots, standing in the basement who just stares at them. This has become so common that the staff has named the spirit Frank. The staff has fun with new employees by sending them down for supplies, and then they laugh when they come back up with a sometimes perplexed, sometimes frightened expression. They simply tell the stunned newbie, "Oh, you just saw Frank."

On the second floor of Evangeline's, in the front, is an area that used to be part of the building next door called the Lady Adams. I was told that staff get an eerie feeling in this section of the store, and one employee began having dreams about it in which they would see an emerald green carpet and casket. There is a prop casket on display here, but it is not the same one the staff member dreamed about. This same person would often hear a disembodied voice speaking to her in Spanish. Many believe that this might have also been Frank. According to the manager, the Lady Adams was built using wood from the first ship to dock along the waterfront, and research showed that one of the crew members of this ship was a Spaniard by the name of Frank. Staff members have also heard their names called out, especially in the stockroom, and footsteps have been heard following the manager, who is always the last one to leave, while they are turning the lights off.

Sacramento may be the capital of California, but as we have only touched the surface of the haunts in and around the city, it may also be the capital for hauntings in California. With so much history, Wild West ambiance, culture and ghosts, I can think of few other places that should go on every paratraveler's vacation itinerary.

The Delta King Hotel

Anyone who has been to Old Sacramento has undoubtedly seen the paddlewheel steamer tied up to the dock in the Sacramento River. This steamer, the *Delta King*, no longer plies the river, but in its heyday, this riverboat and its sister, the *Delta Queen*, sailed up and down the river deltas as well as the San Francisco Bay, not only for the pleasure of its passengers but also to save their lives and serve their country. Today, the *Delta King* serves as a luxury hotel docked along the Sacramento River in Old Town Sacramento.

Both the *Delta King* and *Delta Queen* began their lives in 1924 in Glasgow, Scotland, and then they were disassembled and shipped to Stockton, California, where they were rebuilt and fully fitted out. The California Transportation Company (CTC) spared no expense and spent a whopping $875,000 on each steamboat. The *Delta King* began regular service between San Francisco and Sacramento, leaving from San Francisco on the night of June 1, 1927, while the *Delta Queen* departed from Sacramento; the two boats passed at the midway point, the City of Rio Vista. The entire passage took ten hours and usually took place at night. Unfortunately for the two steamboats and the CTC, the Carquinez Bridge had been opened eleven days earlier, linking San Francisco and Sacramento for a much faster drive between the two cities. Needless to say, this dramatically cut down on both the passenger and freight trade for the CTC.

Once the Great Depression hit, the CTC had to merge with two other companies simply to survive, but with the steamboat trade coming to an

The *Delta King* is an original haunted paddlewheel steamboat.

end, the *Delta King* made its last voyage on September 29, 1940, when it docked in Sacramento. The steamboat wouldn't sit idle for long, as the U.S. Navy acquired the *Delta King* and sailed it to San Francisco, where it became a "receiving" ship (housing for new sailors until they were assigned to their duty ships). After the Japanese attacked Pearl Harbor, the *Delta King* was used as a floating barracks and then as a troop and medical ferry. Once the war was over, it didn't take long before the *Delta King* was decommissioned in 1946. It went through several owners and uses until, finally, the owners of the *Delta Queen*, which was now sailing the Ohio River, bought the *Delta King* for spare parts. The *Delta King* arrived back in Sacramento in 1952. The *Delta King* would never sail under its own power again. The steamboat was beached at high tide and became a landlocked dormitory for the next seven years. In 1959, the steamboat was refloated and towed back to Stockton, where it began a new career. The goal was to turn it into a museum and theater, but a lack of funding and ongoing legal issues put an end to any restoration.

The *Delta King* would go through many legal woes, including the steamship actually being stolen in 1969 and sent back to Sacramento; the thieves, *Riverboat's Comin'*, actually gained the rights to the *Delta King* after the marshals seized it and after a long legal battle. After lawsuits were again filed in 1973, the *Delta King* was once again towed away. This time, the crowd of supporters were told that the *Delta King* was being sent back to San Francisco. But this was simply a story; the *Delta King* was actually being towed into a marsh near Collinsville, California, to be out of sight, out of mind. Here, the *Delta King* became stuck in the mud and flooded up to its freight deck. As the court battles raged, the *Delta King* was refloated and towed to Rio Vista, where it again sat idle while the legal battles continued. The steamboat sank once more and was again refloated in 1982, but this time, investors took notice and began refurbishing the steamboat to be added to the San Francisco Maritime Park. Unfortunately, this never came to fruition, even though renovations were continuing. The legal issues continued until 1989, when finally, the Delta King Hotel opened its doors. Now, the historic *Delta King* is a permanent addition to the Old Sacramento Waterfront. It is hoped that this iconic steamboat and its ghosts will remain for many decades to come.

When talking with employees at the Delta King Hotel, one spirit was always mentioned, that of a former captain. Even though he was mentioned, his existence is not agreed upon by the staff. Those who do believe he is still present say that he is often seen in the pilothouse, seemingly still in command, as the old steamboat once sailed the river. Staff and guests alike have reported seeing the captain walking the decks, checking on his vessel and the comfort of his passengers. He has even been seen "watching" the paddlewheel at the stern, as if making sure the machinery is functioning properly, even though the paddlewheel has not rotated for many years. One of the reasons the crew think this spirit is not real is that reports say the captain is seen standing on the balcony, looking over his ship. This is reported often, even though no balcony exists on the *Delta King*.

What is now a theater on the lower deck of the *Delta King* used to be a morgue during the steamboat's tenure as a troop transport and medical ship. It is not uncommon for guests who are watching a show to get a feeling that they are being watched by unseen eyes. There have even been times when guests suddenly get up and leave the performance to stand outside before returning to their seats. Many have reported that after returning, the feeling no longer hangs over them. They believe that the watcher may have moved on to another patron. Staff I have spoken with have said that every time they have entered the theater, a weird feeling has come over them and remained until they left the room. Staff also told me that they will enter the theater and leave the door open but will watch as the door slowly closes behind them. This does not sound like something paranormal until they mention that the

This page: A night on the *Delta King* is like spending the night with Huck Finn.

door will then open again as they watch. They also mention that, due to the deck being slightly warped, the door always gets stuck on the carpet when it's opened all the way. The door sometimes opens and closes on its own while the employees are standing outside of the theater. This area was not only used as a makeshift morgue; it was also once a section of the boiler room. It is possible, if there is a spirit present here, it could be one of the former crew members who worked in the boiler room. Of course, there may be more than one ghost in this space.

I was shown a video by one of the staff members who said it was a series of pictures they took of their schedule. The schedule was posted on a board, and the crew member, using their phone, snapped a picture of it that they were going to send to their coworker. After looking at the picture, they realized they had the wrong schedule and took another photo of the correct schedule. When sending the photo to their coworker, they found a picture between the two photos of an eerie face staring back at them. The crewmember had taken only two pictures and still cannot explain how the middle picture was on their phone.

The most prevalent stories revolve around a little girl, even though there is no proof of her ever existing. Many believe she was murdered by a "houseman" while traveling on the *Delta King*. There are few employees on the steamboat who do not believe this little girl is haunting the boat. So many things happen to staff that, like the staff aboard the *Queen Mary*, many say you are not an official crew member until the little girl plays with you. It is not uncommon for restaurant staff to place silverware, turn to grab a place setting and find that a fork, spoon or other utensil is missing. The staff then replace the missing implement, only to come back later and find the missing fork next to its replacement.

Carts on the boat will start moving on their own, rolling across the floor and actually picking up speed, trying to keep away from the crew chasing them. Then the carts will stop dead as the staff try not to run into them. The little girl is felt most often down in the restaurant storage room. This room is in the hull of the steamboat, and staff who have been down there alone late at night have said they not only felt like someone is there with them but also saw small shadows darting around and heard the sound of footsteps. This little girl is reported all over the boat, and she may not be alone.

There are surveillance cameras in the museum area of the *Delta King*, and when motion is detected, they will flash green to let staff know that someone is there, hopefully enjoying the displays. I was told that it is not uncommon for these cameras to flash green, yet when staff look at the

The theater on the *Delta King* may be the most haunted spot on the old sternwheeler.

screens, no one can be seen in the museum. The cameras and screens have been checked and rechecked to make sure they are functioning properly, and they always check out. One evening, this mystery may have been solved. One night, after hours, the cameras flashed green, and one of the staff checked the screen to make sure everything was OK. Looking at the cameras, the crew member saw a little girl playing in the museum, and another camera showed multiple figures seemingly playing with her. The strange thing about these other figures is that they didn't look completely solid. While another staff member watched the cameras to keep an eye on the "kids," the other went down to shoo the group back to their rooms. No one was found in the museum space, and the cameras showed that no one had left before they arrived. Staff and guests alike have reported seeing faint footprints walking around the boat, and many believe that this little girl—and possibly her friends—like the *Delta King* because so many new people come aboard for them to meet.

The *Delta King* has seen so much in its lifetime and has a strange connection to Hollywood—the Manson murders and the odd tale of Sharon Tate's premonition (see my book *Ghosts and Legends of Hollywood*) after Paul Bern's wife, Dorothy Mellet, disappeared from the *Delta King*—so it is not a stretch of the imagination to believe the steamship is haunted. As with the ghosts on other haunted steamships and liners, the spirits aboard the *Delta King* are more about having fun and causing mischief and can be an added fun attraction, especially for a paratraveler. So, when in Old Sacramento, I highly recommend a stay at the historic Delta King Hotel.

Ione and Preston Castle

Situated in the beautiful California Gold Country, not far from the hub that is the town of Jackson, sits a dark and foreboding relic of the past. A site built of stone and brick and possible lost dreams. A place where young men went to rehabilitate or move on into a life of crime or, like some, die and "live" out eternity. Known as Preston Castle, the site where many buildings once stood as the Preston School of Industry is now a quiet, brooding place of few structures, dominated by the administration building that eerily resembles a haunted medieval citadel standing as a sentinel atop a small rise. The sinister structure not only looks like a ghost-filled castle, but it also may be, in fact, more haunted than any keep in the world. It is fitting that Preston Castle would have its share of wayward spirits, as it sits near one of Gold Country's most haunted towns. You see, in Ione, California, it is hard to find a place that is spook free.

The small town of Ione had its beginnings in 1849 in California's Gold Country, but unlike most of the other cities and towns in the area, Ione was not a mining town. Mining is not a tool- or material-light endeavor, along with the needed tools, food, clothing and cloth, building materials and other needs for daily life had to be procured, and Ione was the place to get all of these items. Although it's thought to have been named by Thomas Brown after one of the heroines from the drama *The Last Days of Pompeii*, Ione was also known by the names "Bedbug" and "Freezeout" by the miners who worked in the area. Over the next decade, Ione grew with a school, Methodist church, flour mill and the town's first brick building, the Stewart General Store, erected in 1855. This store is still owned by the same family to this day.

By 1876, Ione had grown to have a population of around six hundred folks, including one hundred Chinese residents in Ione's Chinatown. By this time, the town had grown to have six saloons, a brewery, a restaurant, four general stores, one hotel, a meat market and a railroad stop. Ione continued to grow; however, after the gold rush ended and many of the miners headed for more golden pastures, this growth slowed considerably, that is, until the State of California chose Ione for the first Youth Authority installation in the state.

After speaking with many of the locals in Ione, I found that there are quite a few residences that have ghostly activity near the town's downtown area. Some tales I heard were downright frightening. Unfortunately, I don't write about private homes for obvious privacy issues. However, I did find a few stories from some of the businesses on the main street. One comes from the bar across the street from the Ione Hotel. There isn't a whole lot of ghostly activity in this dive bar, but I was told that there is at least one spirit that likes to mess with the bartenders in the lower areas and will, on occasion, play with the patrons. The same can be said for Star Donuts just down the street from the bar and hotel. The donut shop's manager told me that it is not out of the ordinary to hear a young woman greet the employees and customers with a cheerful "hey" or "good morning." The manager even told me that she once heard a disembodied voice singing along to the song on the radio; once the song was over, the voice of the phantom singer faded away. I can tell you from experience that Star Donuts has donuts and food paratravelers won't want to miss. An employee of the Pizza Factory would only say "yes" when I asked if there was any ghostly activity in the pizza joint, but they refused to elaborate when I pressed for specifics.

One place in town that is said to be quite haunted and a favorite place for ghost hunters to stay when visiting Ione and nearby Preston Castle is the Ione Hotel. The hotel was built in 1849 around a well that had originally been built by the Miwok people, who were native to the area. There is a story about a young girl who fell into the well and died, and it's said she's been haunting the hotel ever since. But there is no record of this ever happening, and no one working at the hotel, past or present (that I can find), has ever seen or heard a little girl haunting the Ione Hotel. This is most likely one of those urban legends that has grown to have a life of its own. The reason the hotel was built around the well to begin with was because the hotel wanted water inside the building, rather than outside. As such, the Ione Hotel advertised

The Ione Hotel is your haunt away from home while visiting Preston Castle.

itself as being one of the first hotels in California to have running water. Even though there doesn't seem to be a ghost of a drowned little girl at the hotel, there is most certainly a well-known spirit by the name of George that haunts the building.

I had the pleasure of speaking with the owner of the Burke Family Restaurant, which sits inside the Ione Hotel. Eating at this fine-dining establishment is a must, especially if you are staying at the inn. The owner told me that George was a miner who would come into the hotel nightly to drink and play with the girls from the hotel brothel. (Didn't they all have those?) George didn't try to sleep with or pay for the girls; he just enjoyed their company. It was said that George was a really nice guy and "kind of like your crazy old uncle." It turns out that one night, George had way too much to drink and was in no shape to walk home, so the girls took him upstairs to a room and put him to bed. The next morning, when the girls didn't see George come down nigh on noon, they went up to find him dead from a heart attack. This occurred in what is today's room 13. George is still in the hotel, having a bit of fun.

For those who've stayed in George's room, it is said that he is not all that kind to men who sleep there. He is not mean, yet he lets men know he would prefer a lady's company over that of a man. George has been known to play pranks on men, such as tossing the covers off them in the middle of the night, or if the gentleman is with a lady, he will find that the covers have been removed from him while they are tucked neatly around his companion. Men have also found their shaving kits moved from the bathroom to another place in the room or find them missing completely; on rare occasions, they will find their clothes tossed about the room in a tangled mess. Single ladies, on the other hand, are treated far differently. Girls who sleep in George's room will feel someone get into bed with them, as if they are going to sleep. George is never sexual or in any other way inappropriate with the girls, but they will feel and sometimes hear him sleeping next to them. It is as if George is seeking comfort in his nearness to the fairer sex.

It would also seem that George has a penchant for the game of chess. I was told that, one year, when the hotel and restaurant were decorating for Christmas, one of the decorations was an old chessboard. One day, the restaurateur's husband walked past the board and moved one of the pieces. The next day, upon opening the restaurant, they found that one of the opposing pieces had been moved. Over the next few weeks, George and the owner played an actual game of chess. Sometimes, George would move very quickly, and other times, it could take days. By the way, she refused to tell me who won the game.

It is not clear if this next story is related to George or another spirit in the hotel. One day, a grandfather brought his five-year-old granddaughter into the hotel, just to have a look around. And while talking with a hotel employee, the girl asked her grandfather if he knew the cowboy who was standing behind him. The grandfather asked, "What cowboy?" And he turned around but didn't see anyone standing there. His granddaughter just looked at him and said, "Oh, never mind. He just went into the ceiling in smoke."

Another possible urban legend claims that there is a former brothel madam known as the Black Rose who will sometimes make herself known by manifesting a black rose on room walls. The room where this is seen most is room 7. There is no known historical knowledge of this madam, but the story at the hotel persists. Other occurrences at the hotel include kitchen workers having their names called when no one else is nearby and having their apron strings tugged while working. Ione certainly has its share of paranormal stories, yet they are nothing but a backdrop for one of the most haunted and frightening places in California: Preston Castle.

Preston Castle is one of the very few buildings that remains from the once-prominent Preston School of Industry, and it's the one that always stood out

Star Donuts is a great place for a quick breakfast or a sweet pastry.

as a masterpiece of Romanesque Revival architecture. Today, it stands lonely on a hill, overlooking the town of Ione, dark and foreboding but grand in its beauty. Begun as a way to rehabilitate rather than incarcerate juvenile offenders, the school was also a way to get other wayward boys who, not having broken the law, simply found themselves wards of the state a place to not only receive schooling but also learn a trade. The state, not wanting the new youth facility to look like a prison, began looking around the country for ideas and found the Minnesota State Training School for Boys and Girls in Red Wing, Minnesota. As Preston Castle historian and Foundation President Karl Knobelauch said, California "plagiarized the building to look the same." Construction on the school began immediately, and it was to be dedicated on July 1, 1894; however, the first seven boys arrived in late June.

The castle housed the boys in the basement, and the staff was housed on the second and third floors, with the ground floor turned over to administration and the other floors dedicated as classroom space.

Even though the Preston School of Industry was meant to educate and rehabilitate, the entire school was run like a military school. Those who completed their education would "graduate" with a high school equivalent education (it wasn't until around 1945 that the school was accredited to give out diplomas) and a trade they could use to find work and live a productive life. Living at Preston was not easy, and the fact that the school received juvenile offenders, many of whom were the worst of the worst, made it harder. Knobelauch equated the school at that time to a juvenile Alcatraz. He told me that a few of these youths were so bad that if you put them in a classroom with a pencil, it would not be unusual for them stab another ward with it. These "worst of the worst" would actually be brought into the class in chains, locked up in a cage and only then be given their classroom supplies. By the end of 1895, the school had a student population of 165, and the boys just kept coming.

The original 230 acres that made up the Preston School of Industry grew to become 2,000 acres at its peak. More buildings were constructed to house the growing number of "students," more trades became available as time went on and the Preston School of Industry bordered on self-sufficiency. It raised its own cows, pigs and chickens, which provided not only meat but also milk, eggs and cheese; it grew its own crops; and with the trade shops, it could repair, build and provide other services to the growing school. It even had its own cobbler, which used the leather from the cows to make shoes. Outwardly, the Preston School of Industry looked to be a great success—there were problems, however.

Because Preston was a reformatory, many of the wards didn't want to have anything to do with being there. Since no fence surrounded the school until 1940, it wasn't hard to simply walk away when no one was looking. One of these wards, famous actor Rory Calhoun (Francis Thomas McCown), was sent to Preston at the age of thirteen for a three-year stint. He walked off three times before his sentence was over. He also stole a car and went on a multistate robbery spree, which landed him in Leavenworth and then San Quentin. He was released on his twenty-first birthday and, as luck would have it, fell into a job where his talent (and looks) made him a star in Hollywood. Even after fencing was placed around the school, it didn't work well in deterring the wards from leaving the grounds. Country superstar Merle Haggard was sent to Preston Castle, escaped and was sent back almost immediately by Ione residents who were hoping for a reward. He was eventually sent to San Quentin, where a chance meeting with Johnny Cash (Haggard was in the audience when Cash performed at the prison) turned his life around. Other famous wards of Preston Castle include Beat Generation author Neal Leon Cassady, professional champion tennis player Ricardo "Pancho" Gonzales and rapper Brandt "B-Legit" Jones, to name a few. Not all the wards turned their lives around after graduating from Preston, however.

Although a few wards became famous and highly successful and most went on to lead normal, crime-free lives, there were those who went on to become notorious for high crimes and murder. Jim Quillen may not have been a murderer, but he was eventually sent to Alcatraz Prison in 1942. He was there when another former ward of Preston Castle, Joseph Paul Cretzer, along with Bernard Coy, in an attempt to escape the infamous prison, began what became known as the Battle of Alcatraz. In the end, Cretzer, Coy and another accomplice by the name of Hubbard were killed while hiding in a utility corridor. (For more information on the Battle of Alcatraz, read my book (*Ghosts and Legends of Alcatraz*). Carol Chessman, after being released from Preston Castle, went in and out of prison until he was executed in the gas chamber of San Quentin on May 27, 1960, for robbery, kidnapping and rape; history knows him as the Red Light Bandit.

Perhaps the worst of the worst who was once a ward of Preston Castle was Gerald Gallego. From 1978 to 1980, Gallego and his wife, Charlene (neé Williams), terrorized the Sacramento area, kidnapping young women, mostly teenagers, and then keeping them as sex slaves before killing them and finding new victims. In all, at least ten young girls were raped and murdered by the two killers, who garnered the nickname the "Sex Slave Killers." Although Charlene was eventually paroled, Gerald Gallego died in prison from cancer.

With the State of California sending more and more youths to the Preston School of Industry, more structures were built, and by 1955, the castle was beginning to need more maintenance and was already known to be inadequate for earthquake safety standards at the time. The last of the approximately fifty-five wards who were still living in the castle were moved into other facilities on the property. These boys were part of Company B, who were charged with groundskeeping, housekeeping and culinary arts. As Preston Castle remained the administration building for the school, the staff stayed on until 1960, when, after maintenance costs became too high, they moved into the new administration building farther down the hill. Once

Preston Castle was vacated, the State of California simply ignored the old building. With no maintenance or oversight, the castle began to fall into ruin, with rainwater falling into its interior from the rotting roof. Termites began to infest wooden beams, doors and supports until it became clear that the old administration building needed to be torn down.

The Preston School of Industry remained in operation until 2011. After Governor Ronald Reagan decided that California should stay out of the youth rehabilitation business, the state stopped sending youth to state-run reform schools, along with any money. Preston slowly began to decline until it finally shut its doors for good. The battle for rehabilitating California's youth may have ended, but the battle to save Preston Castle began. Over time, three historically minded women fought the state for the soul of the historic castle, first delaying and then keeping the building from being razed to the ground. Then after the first two foundations were formed and disbanded, the current Preston Castle Foundation came into being in the year 2001, and the dedicated folks of the foundation have been working tirelessly ever since to bring the castle back to its full glory.

After more than forty years of neglect, the castle's roof had all but collapsed, letting rainwater damage much of the interior spaces. The third

Preston Castle in Ione, California.

floor was collapsing, all of the covered wooden porches were in dangerous condition and most of the historic doors that had been termite food needed to be replaced. Because these doors were an odd size and opened in rather than out, they needed to be replaced to follow the fire code. These doors alone cost around $20,000 apiece. The Preston Castle Foundation is brilliant at bringing in the needed funds (although there are those who complain about how they are accomplishing this). The foundation is in the top 2 percent of nonprofits for bringing in funds. There is still a lot of work that needs to be done, and with an estimated $45 million price tag (in today's funds) to complete the restoration, the foundation will continue to get creative in ways to bring in money. Its annual haunted house event at Halloween is its biggest moneymaker, and its history tours are still quite popular. Preston Castle even allows folks to set up their own private paranormal investigations of the castle. Did I mention that Preston Castle is one of the most haunted places in the country? With the history of what went on at the Preston School of Industry, it should come as no surprise that it's haunted. After all, what is paranormal investigating if not delving into the history of the people who lived at the school?

The Preston Castle Foundation president told me that although he is a skeptic, he has had a couple of experiences at the castle that he just can't explain. One took place during one of the castle's movie night events, while the guests were on the back patio enjoying the movie and barbecued hot dogs and hamburgers. Karl said that he and a docent were standing at the bottom of the front steps, keeping an eye on the parking lot, when he heard a "calm, male voice" say his name. As the voice came from directly behind him, he turned, thinking it was a guest or another docent, but he found that there was no one nearby. Confused, he turned back to the person next to him and asked, "Did you hear someone just now?" The other docent said, "Yes, I heard someone call your name." Both Karl and his companion didn't know what to make of the voice, because it was close enough that no one could have gotten out of view before Karl turned around.

Another strange event happened one night when a paranormal group who wanted to film their investigation for their internet followers came to the castle and put on a live telethon investigation to help bring in donations for the castle's restoration. After being on camera to give the telethon audience the history of Preston Castle and making sure the docents who would be working along with the paranormal group had their assignments, Karl headed home for the evening. After a while, Karl tuned into the telethon to check to see how things were going and saw that they were using (as he described it to me) a spirit box to communicate with the ghosts. He said that he had no sooner turned on the live investigation when the spirit box seemed to call out his name. Karl said he immediately called one of his docents to ask if they had heard anything, to which the docent replied, "Yeah, we heard the box call your name." Karl has fun with these odd events and said he figures it is the spirits of Preston Castle getting together and saying to him, "OK, one time, asshole, just one time, we are going to prove to you we are still here."

The dining room seems to be a spot where many of the docents have seen a woman just standing near the opposite end of the room. This occurs after the castle has closed. When the docents try to talk to her to let her know it is time to leave, the figure walks away, turns a corner and simply vanishes. Many wonder if this spirit is that of Anna Corbin. Corbin lived in nearby Ione and worked as head housekeeper at Preston Castle. By all accounts, even though she was not trained as such, she was a mentor and mother figure to the wards who lived at the school. On February 23, 1950, staff member Lillian McDowell found the body of Corbin down in the basement, covered by a rug in the room with the "delousing" pool; Anna Corbin had been beaten to death. The case has never been solved, although nineteen-year-old ward Eugene Monroe was charged with her murder and subsequently released during preliminary hearings due to a lack of evidence. It would not be surprising if Anna is still seeking justice at the castle. However, I was told that the most active place is in the basement near the area known as "intake." The staff at Preston have come to call this spirit the "Old Crabby Guy." They call him this because he dislikes folks coming into the area where he "lives." Some folks have seen him, others have heard him and still others have said they get a strong sense of a "I have to get out of here" feeling, to the point they have to stop themselves from running out of the area. I was told that even guests who have never heard a single story or rumor about the castle being haunted have had strong feelings in this area of the basement.

Many of the docents who have been volunteers at Preston Castle for a long time have become used to experiencing mild, playful pranks as they lead tours or while simply working around the building on restoration. Both staff and guests alike have felt hands on their backs while walking down a hallway, felt a disembodied hand touch their hair, been lightly poked in the back or their side or have felt their ear being tugged. With all of the reports coming from Preston Castle, no one has ever been hurt or felt overly threatened by the spirits that remain here. One former docent told the *San Joaquin Magazine* that "some days the spirits interact and some days they don't." He went on to say that "Preston Castle has…as many stories as square footage to share.…I absolutely believe 100 percent that Preston Castle is haunted."

The docent said that his firm belief comes from the many personal experiences he has had while working at the castle. He said they range from the mild, such as the smell of something cooking coming from the long-cold ovens and seeing a phantom woman in flowing dress walking down the hallway, to actually walking through a male ghost while their eyes are locked on each other. This docent said that he has a "history" with the Old Crabby Guy. "I have seen him multiple times in the intake room as well as the hallway leading to it. I had shone my flashlight down the hall because he was more active than usual and as the beam from my flashlight hit where he was standing the light did not penetrate the black mass and I watched him move up the stairs." He went on to say that the spirit has even stopped him from closing doors. He has also seen many objects "inexplicably move in front of his eyes" and has heard random knocking occur in all parts of the castle.

PARANORMAL STORIES FROM THOSE WHO WORK AT PRESTON CASTLE

MELISSA ZELICO, LEADER OF THE PRESTON CASTLE PARANORMAL TEAM

A few years ago, during one of the castle's Halloween Haunts events, I was with my daughter, Zara, who was seven years old at the time, when I was with two of our scare actors, Tammy and Jerry. I had turned my phone on to help them safely get down the stairs from the second floor; Jerry was the only young boy on the second floor that year, and Melanie, who was in charge of the Boy's Annex Hall, was directly behind me and Zara was in front of me. As we were coming down the stairs, Melanie was enjoying the way Zara and I were scaring guests and getting them to run away from us with very little effort. Melanie could see out of the corner of her eye that someone was behind her, and by the size of the person, she figured it must be Jerry. She began talking to him and was saying things like, "Look at Melissa making those people scream," and, "Isn't it funny how afraid people are of a little kid [Zara]?" Since no response from Jerry was forthcoming, Melanie turned to see if he had heard her but found out that there was nobody there. Melanie freaked out a bit and hightailed it out of there.

I didn't notice any of this going on, because Zara and I were in a "zone," scaring guests and getting them to scream—in other words, having too much fun. A while later during a break between groups, I felt someone standing next to me, and out of the corner of my eye, I could see—or so I thought—Jerry. That is when I heard Tammy and Jerry talking as they were coming back up the stairs. I turned to look at who had come up next to me and could clearly see a boy standing next to me. I looked back at the stairs and then back to the child, and he was gone. He had simply vanished. I let out a scream, ran from behind the curtain I was hiding behind and became quite shaken by the experience. Later, Melanie and I talked about what had happened and were amazed that both of us had the same thing happen at almost the same time and neither of us knew it.

A few years later, also during a Halloween Haunt, I chased a guest down one of the hallways. On my way back to my spot, I noticed feet going up the stairs—no legs or body, just feet. At the same time I saw the feet, three other scare actors, all teenage girls, started to freak out; one was screaming and another was crying because they witnessed these disembodied feet. I asked the girl standing at the bottom of the steps if they had seen anyone go up the stairs. She said no; she had been standing there the entire time, and no one had passed her. I knew the door at the top of the stairs was locked, as I had locked it myself before the event began. We called security, but all they found was a locked door. The three teenage girls refused to stay upstairs after that, and new roles were found for them on the lower floors.

Once, during a "paranormal night," a husband and wife were standing in the east wing hall with me on the second floor. We were facing the room at the end of the hall that, at this time, had a light that would flash off and on. As we watched the light flash on, I could see someone standing there. I turned to the woman next to me and asked if she saw the same thing. She said yes. The light flashed once more, and we could see the figure again. I looked at her, and she just nodded—she had seen it again, too. The light flashed a third time, but now, whatever had been there was gone. This time, the woman ran from the area. Her husband had been looking away and had not seen a thing. A little while later, after the woman had calmed down, we came back up to the second floor, where we had seen the shadow, but now, as we watched, we saw a large black orb fly in a figure eight pattern and then fly down the stairs. That was enough for the woman, who, with her husband, had enough of the second floor for the evening.

Another time during a paranormal night, my group, again on the east wing of the second floor, was engaged in a spirit box session when we saw a shadow figure go into the room at the end of the hall. This was the same room where the husband and wife had watched the big black orb. I asked, "Who are you?" Over the spirit box came the response, "Sam." I asked, "Sam who?" And the same voice responded with, "Sam, Sam Goines." Sam Goines was one of the more well-known wards at Preston Castle. He's buried in the castle cemetery with seventeen other wards.

My last story is about a time I had two teams on the first floor. I left one team in the dining room and went to check in on the other team in the infirmary. As I walked out of the dining room, the team in the room I had just left got an EVP that said, "Melissa!" You can hear my footsteps walking away as the voice says my name. Later, we discovered that both of these teams, each in different rooms but at the exact same time, got EVPs of what sounds like a man screaming, yet no one in either room ever heard a scream.

AARON PLUNK, PRESTON CASTLE PARANORMAL TEAM

When I began volunteering at Preston Castle two years ago, I had never had a paranormal experience and considered myself a nonbeliever. That changed one day while I was working on preparing the castle for its annual Halloween Haunt event.

I had been working on the second floor with Melissa, but when she had to head to the basement to pick up more supplies, I was left alone to continue our work. By this time, most of the doors and windows had been covered with duvetyn, and while I was up on a ladder, I noticed a curtain move as if someone had just walked through it. It was a nice day, and there was no breeze outside. I decided to check to see if someone had come in. As I looked to my left, into the room where Melissa had been working, I saw a very large and heavy (seventy-five-pound) rocking horse moving as if someone was riding it. That is when I heard Melissa coming back up from the basement. She saw the look on my face and asked me what happened. When I told her, she smiled, clapped and congratulated me on having my first paranormal event and becoming a true believer.

JUSTIN DIETEMAN, PRESTON CASTLE FOUNDATION

During a Paranormal Night at the Castle, Francisco Benavides and I arrived early and met up with Melissa in the parking lot. While Melissa went down

One can see why the third floor is sealed off.

to the basement to get things ready for the guests, Francisco and I did a walkthrough of the castle. While on the second floor, we began to hear voices coming from the third floor and people walking around. Since the floor was off-limits, we reported this to Melissa, who said that no one should be up there since the alarm was still on. We couldn't figure out why it wasn't going off. Melissa immediately contacted Karl, the president of the foundation, who told us not to go up there until he arrived (Karl is a retired sheriff). While we waited for Karl, we continued to clearly hear footsteps and talking up above us. After a while, we heard footsteps coming up the main stairway and figured Karl was on his way up, but no one ever appeared. We heard these footsteps repeatedly until Karl, along with an Ione police officer, finally came up to the second floor (they said they had just arrived, so we have no idea who or what was making the other footsteps). The five of us then went up to the third floor to confront the trespassers, but after searching every room on the third floor and even the few rooms we could get to on the fourth floor, we could find no one. The rest of the night was very active, and the paranormal team who had booked the castle had a great investigation that night.

FRANCISCO BENAVIDES, PRESTON CASTLE PARANORMAL TEAM

The first paranormal experience I had at Preston Castle actually occurred during my first investigation there. The docent that night suggested that I walk the second floor by myself without a light so I could get a feel for the place. I was a bit braver back then, so I didn't hesitate to do it. Justin Dieteman (who had gotten me involved in investigating) was photographing the apartment on the same floor but on the opposite side of the castle. When I got to the end of the hall I had been walking down, this overwhelming feeling of dread came over me. It was something I had never felt before. I turned around and picked up the pace, heading to where Justin was, and I began to hear footsteps coming up behind me. I stopped and turned around, but nothing was there. I continued walking, and the footsteps continued. Every time I looked behind, there was still nothing there. I began to panic but then saw Justin, who snapped a picture as I came closer. The picture he took caught something behind me that neither of us could see. I always felt that there was a spirit of someone in authority on the second floor, and since that night, I have seen many shadow figures on the second floor. This figure, however, felt very intense, and I have run into him many times as well.

Jeremy Monson, Preston Castle Paranormal Team

I had been in charge of changing a large room we call Company B into something we could use for a charity haunt event to raise money for the ongoing restoration of the castle. One of the things I created was an area with enlarged, old-style toys, like the old "Jacks" game. After the event was over, it was my job to change the room back to its original configuration and clean out all of the changes. I was almost finished doing this and was holding onto one of the large rubber balls we had used (similar to a dodgeball) while looking down the long seventy- to eighty-foot hallway. I thought to myself, "I wonder if I could bowl this ball all the way down to the T at the end." So, of course, I did. What was odd, however, was that when the ball reached the T, it stopped dead in the middle of the intersection. Then as I watched, it turned left. I figured there must have been a breeze that blew it down the other hallway, but as soon as I thought that, the ball rolled back and headed down the other direction, in the T and out of sight. This was sort of weird and kinda spooky, so I went to get the ball and called it a day.

Renee Richardson, Preston Castle Paranormal Team

I had been invited to a docent-only night investigation at the castle, and while on the second floor with a few other investigators, we were in the hallway looking toward the apartment at the end of the hall. At the same exact time, Francisco (another docent) and I both noticed and spoke up about a dark shadow we saw peeking out of the left side of the doorway at the end of the hall. We then saw a second shadow peeking out of a closet, which was much closer to us in the hall. These were my first shadow figures, and having it validated by another seasoned investigator was really cool.

☠ ☠ ☠

The history of Preston Castle is one of redemption, loss and, on occasion, violence and murder, but its legacy is written in its successes. With its influential writers, poets and sports figures, along with famous musicians and movie stars, Preston Castle has produced more successes than failures. What it takes to teach and guide troubled youth into becoming productive citizens is patience and, as it has been said of Anna Corbin, "a kindness and love to lead the way." There are stories out there about the castle torturing, abusing and mistreating the wards under the care of the Preston staff. I'm sure there have been a case or two of this happening, but I could find no legitimate history or official reports of this occurring en masse. Preston Castle has been featured in many movies, such as the film *Asylum* (supposedly based on

The accommodations for the wards were spartan at best.

"true" stories, but...), as well as the movie *A Haunting at Preston Castle*, along with numerous paranormal TV "reality" shows. So many of my readers have mostly seen and heard about the location, but very little is known about the true history of the castle. Regardless of what knowledge the paratraveler has, this is one location that should go near the top of your bucket list. And don't forget, one can stay close by and dine in Ione at the haunted Ione Hotel while visiting these locations.

Jackson, the Kennedy Mine and the Amador County Courthouse

The town of Jackson, California, is the Amador County seat, and like most Gold Country towns, it was born and grew up out of the Coloma gold rush. Jackson, however, grew to become one of the most important cities in the area, and after losing prominence as the seat of government for Calaveras County, it fought tooth and nail for the honor of filling that role for the new county of Amador. Jackson began life with the name Botellas, Spanish for "bottles," in 1848. (The reason for the name has been lost to time.) But after the gold rush and more easterners flooded in, the town changed its name to Jackson. The town, like many, was filled with gambling halls, saloons, brothels and a famous live oak hanging tree, and although it was not completely lawless, these staples of Wild West gold mining towns caused a bit of a ruckus. Bloodshed, violence and drunken rapes permeated the early years of the fledgling city. This type of activity may be one of the reasons the city of Jackson is so haunted.

Today, Jackson is a beautiful and historic town, and a stroll down its charming main street can almost make one feel they have traveled back in time. Antique stores, cafés, eateries and bars line both sides of the street, and many still play host to the residents of the past. One of these places is the Mother Lode Deli. Here, you find coffee, pastries, sandwiches and specters—well, at least one specter. According to the servers I spoke with, the spirit that resides at the deli seems to be interested only in those who work there, although diners have noticed strange things. One of them told me that she had been working one day, preparing guest's drinks, when she felt

The National Hotel in Jackson may be one of the most haunted in California.

someone standing behind her. Just as she was finishing up, she felt a brush on her arm, as if someone had just passed, but no one was there. She went on to say she let out a startled squeak. The other server I was talking with started laughing and said, "Oh, yeah, I was there and remember that." They both said that they believe the spirit is that of their former boss Alma Garcia, because the things the spirit does always seem to revolve around making sure they are doing things correctly.

Another eatery on the street is Rosebud's Café. Here, the owner told me that in the more than thirty-four years she has owned the café, she and those who work for her never feel alone in the restaurant, even when they are alone. She stated that working at night, folks and staff will see things out of the corners of their eyes, but when they look, there is nothing there. There is a stage for musicians in the front corner of the café, and she told me that twice she has been called over to diners' tables to be told that they sensed her mother standing on stage, surveying the café and sending out a vibe that conveys how proud she is of her daughter for what she has created.

Jackpot Jen's Vintage is an antique store, and Jen told me that the store is her "happy place." One of the reasons for this is what she believes to be the feelings of kindness put out by the spirit that dwells within the shop. Jen said that when she moved in, the former owner told her that she may hear footsteps up in the false attic but was told not to worry, as whoever was up there was not dangerous. Over the years, Jen has certainly come to agree. She said that a dress she had on display increased the good feelings in the shop, and they remained even after she donated the dress to a museum. It goes to show that not all ghosts—or even most—are scary. They are just misunderstood. There is even a bar in town called the Main Event that has a spirit that can mimic anyone's voice and likes to have a bit of fun with patrons.

Jackson has a long and storied mining past, having begun during the California Gold Rush. As such, two of its mines, the Kennedy and the Argonaut, top them all for their histories and storied pasts. Unfortunately, their fame came at the cost of forty-seven miners. The Kennedy Gold Mine began in 1860, shortly after Irish immigrant Andrew Kennedy discovered a quartz outcropping near what is today Highway 49, leading into the town of Jackson. Operating off and on over the next few years, the mine closed in 1878 but was reopened in 1886 after investors formed the Kennedy Mining and Milling Company. New shafts were dug; one of these was the east shaft, which reached a depth of 5,912 feet. This shaft became the deepest vertical gold mine in North America. As the dawn of the twentieth century arrived, the Kennedy complex grew, but in 1928, a fire broke out in one of the buildings and all of the structures, only the stamp mill and the main office, survived. Other than these two structures, every building we see today was built after 1928.

When, in 1942, the federal government shut the gold mines down as "nonessential" in favor of those mines that were producing ore needed for the war effort, the Kennedy Mine had produced roughly $34.3 million worth of gold ore, with over 95 percent of investors' dividends being paid out at $20.67 an ounce, a fortune today. After the war, a halfhearted attempt was made to reopen the mine, but the funds needed to restart the mining operations were deemed to be more costly than the expected return. The Kennedy Mine property remained abandoned until 1961, when a San

An original ore cart at the Kennedy Mine.

Francisco teacher by the name of Sybil Arata bought the entire property for $41,600 at a liquidation sale and moved into the manager's office, where she lived for many years. With her death in 1994, Sybil's will stated that the property should be kept open as a wildlife habitat, and what was left of the Kennedy Mine was to be maintained for its historical value.

The Kennedy Mine is not the only historic mining operation that sprang up in Jackson. The Argonaut Mine, once one of the highest gold-producing mines in California, became famous not for its mining but for its mining disaster. The Argonaut, or, as it was first named, the Pioneer Mine, was discovered by two freed slaves, William Tudor and James Hager, and the friends laid claim to the mine in the 1850s. They then began seeking their fortunes. In the 1860s, the two men sold their claim for $5,000 to the Pioneer Gold & Silver Mining Company. This company kept the mine until 1893, when it, in turn, sold the operation to the Argonaut Mining Company. After the company bought the mine and changed its name to the Argonaut, mining operations stepped up. This mine became one of the biggest producers and the second-richest mine in California by 1922. That same year, the Argonaut also produced the worst mining disaster in California history.

On August 27, 1922, a fire broke out in the lower levels of the Argonaut Mine. Forty-seven men were working their late shift almost a mile

Argonaut Mine disaster, Jackson, California. Volunteers made it possible for the Amador County chapter, American Red Cross, Jackson, California, to meet all demands during the Argonaut Mine disaster relief work. Three machines in the motor service that carried supplies to families of the entombed men and also carried cooked dishes to the canteens for rescue workers. California, United States, Jackson, 1922. Photograph. *Library of Congress, https://www.loc.gov/item/2017680003.*

underground when they realized what was happening, but by then, their route to safety had been cut off. The miners who had been working closer to the adit (the mine's entrance) managed to get clear and sound the alarm. What happened next was a nightmare for the miners and townsfolk, and it played out over the next twenty-two days. As the Kennedy and Argonaut Mines were so close to each other—even with the sometimes-hostile rivalry between the two (there was even an unsubstantiated rumor that a Kennedy Mine worker started the fire)—the Kennedy began digging a tunnel opening from one of its shafts to the adjoining Argonaut shaft in an effort to rescue the trapped miners.

It took two days for the fire to be extinguished, and by then, word of the catastrophe had spread nationwide, with reporters, news teams and celebrities coming into Jackson to lend any support they could. With two teams working around the clock to reopen the two tunnels between the mines that had been closed off since a 1919 fire, the American Red Cross came to town to care for the rescue workers. The entire effort was now being watched around the world. After three weeks, crews reached the area where they believed the trapped miners were located. They knew it was now a recovery effort, and forty-seven coffins had already arrived. So, when they found a makeshift bulkhead that the other miners had built to try to survive the fire and accumulating poisonous gas, they were not surprised to find the bodies of the dead miners in the small area where they had gathered. What did surprise them was that they found only forty-six bodies, not forty-seven.

According to Kennedy Mine historians, the rescuers found writing on the wall of the alcove where the Argonaut miners perished; it read, "3 o'clock, gas getting strong." Another said, "3:15, half knocked out." And the last one, which was never finished, simply said, "4 o'clock, Fessel…" Fessel was the one miner who was not found with the forty-six bodies. Speculation ran the gamut from Fessel being a hero who went looking for a way to save himself and the others to Fessel being the one who started the blaze. In the long run, Fessel's body was found just over a year later in an area distant from where his fellow miners were found. It seems that Fessel may have been checking on the flooding from both the natural accumulation of water and the water used to extinguish the blaze.

With so much human death from accidents, natural causes and other factors that took place at these two competing mines, it is no wonder that folks talk about how haunted the mines are. It also seems, perhaps due to the connecting shafts, those spirits from the Argonaut are also found visiting the Kennedy Mine. Ghost hunter Vicky Galloway said that during an investigation of the Kennedy Mine, they had a few interesting things happen. Vicky said that at the very start of the night, she witnessed a shadow figure on the grass as they were being given their safety meeting; it was still daylight when this happened. Later, while the group was sitting on the balcony of the mining office, they saw another shadow figure walk into the room where a safe is kept. When they went to look, they saw a figure with "long fingernails" trying to close themselves into the vault. At this same moment, Vicky heard the docents shouting, and when they looked outside, they saw another shadow figure darting across the lawn before it vanished.

Shadow figures aren't the only spirits found at the old mining office. During my tour, the docent told us that once, during filming at the office, two of the film crew ran down, all excited, to say that the ghost of Teresa, the spirit of a woman who once lived there, told them that she had once owned a boardinghouse and that her granddaughter now owns a restaurant. They couldn't have known that the granddaughter of Teresa does in fact own a restaurant in town.

Another ghost hunter, Ann Bender, told me that during an investigation of a home, near where the families of the Argonaut victims waited for news of their loved ones, one of their pieces of equipment began tapping out

Left: Teresa is one of the spirits at the Kennedy Mine.

Opposite: Prisoners scrawled their names in odd places in the jail.

"SOS" at 10:45 p.m., and this lasted until 11:00 p.m. They found out later that this period coincided with the time the fire began and the power went out in the mine. The Kennedy Mine is certainly a place the paratraveler should have on their list of haunted locations to visit.

Another historic location in Jackson that allows investigations is the old Amador County Courthouse and Jail. Originally built in 1854, this wooden structure, like many in Gold Country, succumbed to the ravages of flame. Rebuilt in 1864 using brick, the courthouse was connected to the hall of records, which was built next door in the 1930s, by a catwalk on the second floor, while the ground level was used as an outdoor area for the jail's inmates. In 1940, the buildings were fully incorporated into each other, and the familiar Art Deco façade seen today was added. The courthouse and jail were in continuous use from 1864 to the early 2000s, when it was decommissioned due to ADA requirements. Today, after sitting

empty and abandoned in the middle of historic Jackson for almost twenty-three years, the property is being restored by Jamie and Patrick Macklin as a museum and event venue. Since they've restored the old courthouse and had numerous paranormal episodes occur, they now allow investigators to come and explore the eerie happenings of the building.

There are carvings in the cell walls that give glimpses into the history of the jail. One is a carving that says "Kentucky Brothers," and one in the women's cell reads, "Margie and Jackie 1959." There is a murder confession from two wards who killed a victim by the name of James A. Wieden, an instructor at the Preston School of Industry. And found in the archives are documents of deaths by suicide and strange hangings of prisoners in their cells. One of these prisoners, Bogdan Masanovich, was found in cell 13 in 1887. These could be the reasons that, over the years, Jamie and Patrick have noticed extreme temperature changes while walking from one room to another, the feeling of someone brushing up against them when no one is there and the sound of slamming doors in the otherwise empty building. Other visitors have said they have heard spectral jail guards running their nightsticks along the bars as they make their rounds, and during investigations, the same piece of equipment, regardless of the team doing the investigation, will always produce a woman's voice.

Ann Bender, who used to give tours of the Amador County Courthouse, said that one evening, she and her husband were investigating there, and

The jail, like the building itself, has Art Deco influences.

every time she glanced outside, she would see a white flash zoom by as if something had been watching through the window. She said that it was as if a person dressed in a sheet was flying past. She said that same night, the first time she ever investigated the courthouse, the number of EVPs she collected was enormous. On another investigation, this time with two law enforcement officers, one of the investigators from her team was chased by what they described as a "black mist." When the officers heard this, they went to inspect the area and came back to say that one of them had been scratched by an unseen force. The team went down to where all of this occurred and called out to who or whatever might have been there, but no response was forthcoming—until one of the team members was suddenly scratched on her back. The investigator described getting scratched, saying it felt like a "burning sensation."

A similar event happened later that night, when a team member who was in the courtroom felt a presence behind her. She turned and saw a solid black mist form in front of her. The investigator said the mist was so dense that not even a cop's tactical flashlight could penetrate the blackness. Suddenly, loud footsteps could be heard running directly at her, and before she could react, the black mist flew at and through her. Ann said that she decided to end the investigation at that point, admitting that in over twenty years of giving tours, this was the only time she had to "pause" an investigation. Say what you will, but it would seem there are spirits at the old courthouse and jail. And they are certainly, if not nice, a bit on the violent side. Of course, considering who they were in life and where they choose to spend their afterlife, this does not come as a surprise.

THE USS *HORNET*

The USS *Hornet* began life as the USS *Kearsarge* on August 3, 1942. However, when the USS *Hornet*, CV-8, was sunk on October 26, 1942, during the Battle of Santa Cruz Island, CV-12 had its name changed from *Kearsarge* to *Hornet*. To this day, the name *Kearsarge* is still proudly stamped on the *Hornet*'s keel. *Hornet* was one of the twenty-four famed Essex-class aircraft carriers built during World War II and was also one of the most decorated ships in the U.S. Navy. Able to carry up to one hundred aircraft, it also had a dizzying array of antiaircraft and antiship guns, ranging in size from twenty millimeters up to five-inch/.38-caliber guns. In all, sixty-two guns protected the ship and its aircraft. With a full complement of men and machines, it displaced 36,380 tons and had a range of twenty thousand nautical miles. Eight boilers powered four Westinghouse geared steam turbines, turning four propellers that gave the ship an impressive thirty-three knots, or approximately thirty-eight miles per hour.

After a full training schedule with shakedown cruises in the Atlantic, the *Hornet* finally headed out to the Pacific Ocean and into the fight against the Empire of Japan. Arriving at Pearl Harbor, the *Hornet* took on its airwings and provisions and headed out into harm's way on March 15, 1944. For the next fifteen months, the USS *Hornet* would perform combat operations, first in New Guinea, supporting MacArthur's campaign, and then it went on to the Mariana Islands and, finally, Truk Island. After a brief port call, the *Hornet* headed out for the Great Marianas Turkey Shoot, the name given to the Battle of the Philippine Sea due to U.S. Navy aviators destroying what

USS *Hornet*, CV-12. Its namesake, CV-8, launched the Doolittle Raid against Tokyo.

remained of the Japanese naval air forces. After the Turkey Shoot, the *Hornet* remained to support the landing troops. USS *Hornet* then moved on to the Battles of Iwo Jima and Okinawa, at one point coming within forty miles of the Japanese home islands to participate in a naval blockade and aerial bombardment. USS *Hornet* was badly damaged by a typhoon in late June 1945 and had to return to the United States for repairs, by which time, the war with Japan was over.

During its time in combat, the *Hornet* came under air attack fifty-nine times, but no bomb could ever get through its screen. The F6F Hellcat fighters of the USS *Hornet* hold the record for most enemy aircraft shot down in a single day (72) and the record for most destroyed in a month (255). The *Hornet* also holds the record for the most enemy aircraft shot down in the air (668). Its 1,410 enemy aircraft destroyed is surpassed only by the USS *Essex*. Ten fighter pilots from the *Hornet* became "aces in a day," a record that may never be broken. Pilots from the USS *Hornet* sank a total of 1,250,000 gross tons of shipping and played a vital role in the sinking of the Japanese super battleship *Yamato*. Countless U.S. Marines and soldiers were also saved by its close air support and other units.

Due to the damage the *Hornet* sustained during the June 1945 typhoon, twenty-five feet of its flight deck collapsed. So, the *Hornet* made a brief stop in the Philippines and then headed to Alameda, California, for repairs. The *Hornet* arrived in early July, and its overhaul was completed by September 13, 1945. With the war over, the job of repatriating hundreds of thousands of U.S. service personnel back to the United States fell squarely on the U.S. Navy. USS *Hornet* sailed from Alameda, heading back to the Pacific theater of operations as part of "Operation Magic Carpet." This time, however, in what was called "the best missions of the war," CV-12 carried troops from the Marianas and Hawaii back home to their wives and families. Once the operation was over, the *Hornet* sailed home to San Francisco, arriving on February 9, 1946. USS *Hornet* was decommissioned there on January 15, 1947. Although the ship was placed in the Pacific Reserve Fleet, it wouldn't remain there for long.

On March 20, 1951, the *Hornet* was recommissioned and sailed from Alameda, California, to the New York Naval Shipyard. Once the carrier arrived, it was again decommissioned and entered drydock, where it was converted into an attack aircraft carrier. Once the conversion was complete, USS *Hornet* was recommissioned CVA-12 and then headed to the Caribbean Sea for extensive training for its new role. On May 11, 1954, the *Hornet* departed Norfolk Naval Station for operations in the Mediterranean Sea and the Indian Ocean before joining the Seventh Fleet in the South China Sea. There, on July 25, aircraft from the *Hornet*'s task group shot down two attacking communist Chinese fighter planes. USS *Hornet* would go on to help cover the evacuations of Vietnamese from advancing communist forces and perform patrol duties before entering the Puget Sound Naval Shipyard in January 1956 for the installation of an angled flight deck and other improvements. After returning to the Seventh Fleet, the *Hornet* once again entered drydock from January to July 1958 to be converted to an antisubmarine warfare support carrier. USS *Hornet* would emerge from drydock as CVS-12. USS *Hornet* continued sailing with the Seventh Fleet and patrolled the waters off the coast of Vietnam in support of U.S. troops through much of 1967. USS *Hornet* was decommissioned for the last time on June 26, 1970, and it spent the next two decades in mothballs. It looked like the famed carrier was destined for the scrapyard.

USS *Hornet* had a stellar career as one of America's premier aircraft carriers, but it was also an integral part of NASA and the United States' race to the moon. After the success of the Mercury and Gemini space missions, the Apollo space program, already in the testing phase, ramped up with a mandate to have an American walk on the moon by the end of the 1960s. Mercury proved the ability of a single human to operate in space, and with

President Nixon congratulates *Apollo 11* astronauts through the window of the mobile quarantine van located in the hangar deck, July 24, 1969. *National Archives no. 428-kn-18088; USS* Hornet, *Puget Sound Naval Shipyard, Sinclair Inlet, Bremerton, Kitsap County, WA; photos from Survey HAER WA-34.*

Gemini moving into a larger space vehicle that could accommodate two men, tests for an even larger, three-man space capsule were already in the works. On August 25, 1966, the *Hornet* took station near Wake Island in the Pacific Ocean. There, the carrier hoisted one of the first unmanned Apollo spacecraft aboard, which had just rocketed three-quarters of the way around the Earth in ninety-three minutes. Then, on July 24, 1969, USS *Hornet* was again on station in the Pacific Ocean to recover the *Apollo 11* astronauts after their historic first walk on the moon. One more time, the USS *Hornet* headed out nine hundred miles west of Hawaii to recover the *Apollo 12* crew and spacecraft. The *Hornet* would recover more spacecraft and astronauts than any other ship in history.

Although it was laid down as the USS *Kearsarge*, the *Hornet* would go on to become one of the most famous—and arguably most important—United States aircraft carriers in history. After its decommissioning, the carrier languished for twenty-nine years before it was finally stricken from the Naval Vessel Registry on July 25, 1989. And although it was added into the National Historic Landmark Registry in 1991, the ship was almost sold for scrap and scheduled to be sent to the breakers in April 1993. Luckily, a group stepped forward with a plan to save this great piece of American history, and the navy donated the ship to The Aircraft Carrier *Hornet* Foundation as an air and space museum on May 26, 1998. Today, CVS-12 USS *Hornet* proudly sits as a reminder of America's greatness in Alameda, California, where thousands of folks come each year to learn about the U.S. Navy carrier forces, the NASA Space program and naval aviation while touring a truly remarkable naval vessel. The entire museum is run by a great staff of volunteers, and it is said that many of the men who served aboard the ship in its World War II days remain, even though they are no longer among the living.

USS *Hornet*, having been involved with some of the deadliest naval battles of World War II, as well as the inherent dangers of launching and recovering aircraft, both propeller-driven and jet-powered, had many men killed and wounded during battle, in accidents and, unfortunately, by suicide. Regardless of the reasons these men were killed, they all had one thing in common: they were all dedicated and devoted patriots who took their duty of protecting America and its citizens as their sacred vow. Because of this devotion, many of the crew who have passed away have remained aboard CV-12 to help maintain not only the ship but also the hard-fought rights of the people who live in the United States of America.

Over the years the ship has served as a museum, so many reports of ghost sightings have come from the USS *Hornet* that the ship has become known as the "most haunted ship in America." I have had the pleasure of participating in an overnight investigation of this magnificent aircraft carrier and had a few interesting things happen during the evening. While in the forecastle, a group of us were engaged in an EVP (electronic voice phenomenon) session when one among our group spotted someone coming out of the secondary navigation bridge. The woman pointed the gentleman out to the rest of us, and at first, we thought it might be one of the overnight crew members who was staying aboard as fire watch. We all noticed that the man was wearing an officer's uniform and seemed to be walking toward the ladder that would bring him down to our level. The man paid no attention to us, and when he reached the ladder, he simply vanished from sight. This was the first time I had ever seen an actual apparition. Later in the evening, as we were getting ready for bed, we began hearing talking coming from the medical ward. Since our bunks were directly next to medical, we figured that it was other folks from our overnight group. However, we found on investigating that there was nobody in medical, and the voices could still be heard while we were there in the room. One more thing that occurred that night is something that we had thought was a joke from ship's staff. We were told that the berthing area we had picked had an odd tendency to mess with guest's shoes. We were told that shoes would be moved around in the berthing area so that guests had to go looking for them later. We found out in the morning that this was no joke, and most of us had a scavenger hunt waiting for us when we woke up.

Our group is by no means the only one who has seen spirits in the area of the forecastle and battle bridge. California Institute of Technology (Caltech) in Pasadena, California, has a page on its website dedicated solely to ghost stories from the USS *Hornet*. A man by the name of Ryan

A ship's officer is sometimes seen here outside the auxiliary bridge.

Garrett, who worked on CV-12, mentioned an incident very similar to the one my team experienced.

> *While working the live aboard* [overnight] *program, we tell ghost stories in the forecastle. Every now and then one of the other crew members will put on a sailor's uniform to scare the kids. One night, as the uniformed crewman walked out of the bullnose* [bridge] *I saw another man in a sailor's uniform behind him. He was only there for a split second and then vanished. Later in the month, during a different live aboard, I saw the same man on the catwalk, once again the man vanished into thin air.*

Could this have been the same sailor my team, Planet Paranormal, saw during our stay?

Many guests and crew say that the medical bay is the haunted heart of the USS *Hornet.* This is due to the amount of paranormal activity reported in and near the ship's hospital facilities. Also found on the Caltech website is a tale shared by Steven Shirk. According to Shirk, he had come to the *Hornet* on a 4H Exchange Club trip with his host family and took a lot of pictures while touring the ship. He said that when he got back home, he was looking at his photos and found a picture he thought was rather odd. It was one of the ones he had taken while in the "medical wing." In the photo was a chair he knew was empty at the time he snapped the picture, but now, as he looked at the image, he could see someone sitting there. He said that the figure seemed to be wearing an "old-time pilot's" helmet and looked to be tied down. He said he showed it to the people who were on the trip with him, and they all saw the same thing—but not while they were there. He said that just thinking about that picture sends chills up his spine. Being tied to the chair and wearing an aviator's helmet, could this be the spirit of a Japanese prisoner who, once brought aboard, went insane and died and has been seen ever since?

Another story from the Caltech site states that a guest named Megan didn't know the ship's haunted reputation when she came aboard with her uncle. But like Steven in the previous story, her uncle decided to take lots of pictures while touring. While looking through the pictures they took in the hospital, she came across one showing the X-ray machine. The machine was obviously switched on, as you could clearly see the light on the screen. Another thing you can see in the photo is that the cord for the X-ray machine is not plugged into the outlet. Megan also came across a picture showing what looks to be a person lying on one of the hospital beds. The figure is that of a shadow, and you can see the indent on the bed, as if the shadow figure has weight. She and her family looked at the picture for quite a while and then decided to check the internet, where they found some "scary stories" about the ship. After reading some of the ghost stories, Megan went back to take another look at the photograph, and this time, there was also an axe lying on the bed that hadn't been in the picture the last time she and her uncle had looked at it. Another strange

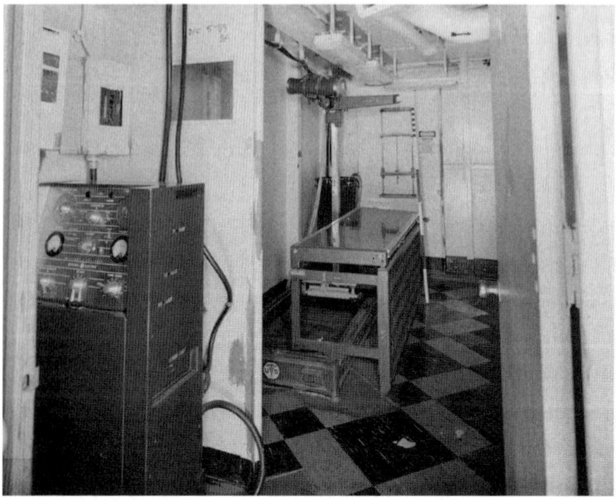

Medical department, X-ray room; aft looking forward, showing a portable X-ray unit. *USS* Hornet, *Puget Sound Naval Shipyard, Sinclair Inlet, Bremerton, Kitsap County, WA; photos from Survey HAER WA-34.*

thing about this is that her uncle never snapped a picture while in the medical ward. It's as if the camera had taken the picture without "living" human assistance.

USS *Hornet*, CV-12, also has your standard ghost stories about hatches that slam shut on their own, doors that open and close with no human hand to aid them, spectral voices in conversation about everything from the war effort to girlfriends, wives and families back home. Many folks find these stories frightening; others have become so scared by spirit events that they refuse to set foot on the decks ever again. Still others refuse to believe what their own eyes are telling them and think it is the ship itself trying to promote its ghost tours. One thing I do know: as someone who has had the pleasure of working aboard another haunted warship museum, those spirits that have remained after death have nothing but honorable intentions and a wish to keep the history of the ship, the U.S. Navy and the memory of those who died in the service of their country alive for future generations.

Alcatraz Island

Long before the waters of the Pacific Ocean filled what is now San Francisco Bay, the Ohlone tribes called the area around Alcatraz home. At that time, Angel Island and Alcatraz Island were mountains that were hunted by the various tribes, and the trees there were used for firewood. When the waters of the Pacific claimed the lower sections of the mountains, the Ohlone simply moved and continued life in what is now known as the Bay Area.

The Ohlone tribes lived in relative peace with each other, and they worshipped the spirits of the plants, the animals and Mother Earth. To them, life was a cycle of birth, death and rebirth, a great circle that was interdependent on all living things. As an Ohlone explained it, "We die, the grass grows, the rabbit eats the grass, the birds eat the rabbit and then we become a part of everything; the trees, bushes, rabbits and birds, even the ocean itself." The Ohlone not only had their benevolent spirits; they also had malevolent spirits, and one of the worst lived on Alcatraz Island.

The Ohlone had used Alcatraz for hundreds of years as a fishing base. They also used the island as a prison for undesirable members of the tribe who had broken tribal law. The only way to travel to and from Alcatraz was by boat, so those who had offended the tribe were taken to the island and left there. The Ohlone would bring out needed supplies and water and then depart; they would spend as little time there as possible because of the evil spirits and the ghosts of ancestors that couldn't find their peace in death that lingered there. They also believed that those imprisoned on the island who

Historic American Buildings Survey, creator, and Joseph A. Baird. *Alcatraz, San Francisco Bay, San Francisco County, California, 1933; documentation compiled after, photograph; Library of Congress, https://www.loc.gov/item/ca0622.*

had died there would come back to seek revenge for their banishment and untimely death as a Bukwus.

Evil entities were said to walk the shores of Alcatraz, and though it was a stop for fishing and place of rest, no one would venture farther than the waterline, even to bury those deemed unworthy of a funeral pyre or rituals conducted by the shamans to keep evil away from fishermen who plied the waters near the island. The worst of the evil were the savage, human-like, undead drowning victims that appeared as hairy, bloated, decaying corpses. The Bukwus possess great physical strength and can become invisible to get close to their victims. Because they are the tortured souls of those who have drowned and been turned by other Bukwus, they can be found anywhere there is a body of water where people have drowned.

One of the traits of the Bukwus is that they try to take the living to turn them into Bukwus. They offer the living a cockle shell filled with ghost food, and if the living person is foolish enough to eat from the shell, they are turned into a Bukwus. If the person refuses to eat the food, the Bukwus attempt to drown them to condemn them to an afterlife of eternal hunger, misery and wandering at the side of the Bukwus.

After the United States acquired Alta California, the government took control of the islands within San Francisco Bay. Washington, D.C., then implemented a plan of coastal defense that would become known as the Plan of 1850. The plan called for fortifications on both the north and south shores of the harbor entrance to catch incoming enemy ships in a crossfire, along with a third fortification inside the harbor on Alcatraz. The construction of these forts began in 1853. Alcatraz was the first completed by a good five years, and it had the first permanent American guns, seven eight-inch and one ten-inch, placed on the Pacific coast.

When the American Civil War began, the army built up Alcatraz with smaller and cheaper earthwork batteries that could house the new rifled cannons that were being installed at the other fortifications around the bay. Along with the added fortifications, Alcatraz was to be used as a prison for deserters, malcontents and Confederate prisoners of war.

The prison that was in use at this time was nothing more than a square cement holding tank underneath one of the sally ports. It was as sparse as a room could be and was often crowded with more prisoners than it could humanely house. It was cold and drafty, and many of those interred here came down with sicknesses and maladies that often went untreated and ultimately killed them. When a tuberculosis outbreak occurred in the prison "hole," the inmates began to die, and as the disease spread, nurses from San Francisco volunteered to come to the island to treat them. One of these nurses unfortunately contracted the disease and was not allowed to leave the island. They wouldn't even allow her to leave the prison room. The nurse died from her ailment, locked up and alone, save for the criminals she had vowed to save. This brave soul is still trapped at Alcatraz to this day and is often heard in the sally port above the original cell.

As the 1900s dawned, Alcatraz was declining as a military base, but it was growing as a prison facility. It was at this time that strange stories began being told by the military personal who still manned the island. One of the first reports came in 1902, when a trooper reported hearing drums while on watch. The trooper stated that as he approached the parade grounds, the drums got louder and louder until he reached the area where he thought the noise was coming from. The trooper said he cautiously walked onto the parade grounds, and the drums suddenly stopped. The man looked around but found no one and never heard the drums beating again.

During World War II, Alcatraz was used as a torpedo and mine storage location. After a late-night restocking ship dropped off a new supply of ordinance, the men began stacking and storing new torpedoes. Suddenly, all five of the men began hearing the sound of drums. The sound was coming from the docks, and the men wondered if the scow was playing some odd drum music over the radio. As they approached the docks, they began to hear the sound of chanting in unison with the drumming. Rounding a corner, they stopped dead in their tracks; there in front of them was a campfire. The drumming was coming from Natives who were sitting around a fire while others danced around the pit. The soldiers moved forward to tell the Natives that they were violating federal law by being on Alcatraz, but before they could take three steps, the entire scene vanished before their eyes. According

Below the grate in this sally port lies the original prison of Alcatraz.

to one trooper, the only reason they reported the incident was to make sure they didn't get in trouble for leaving their assigned task. The legends of the phantom drums and drummers started to come in more frequently as the war ended and the military ended all use of the island. Over the years, guards and prisoners alike have reported hearing the drums playing, and the dancers were seen by both prison guards and park rangers after the prison was closed down.

After Alcatraz was turned over to the Federal Prison Authority, reports of apparitions within the prison itself began to grow. As with all prisons, violence and death were ever present at Alcatraz; this has a tendency to leave an imprint in the ether and cause paranormal activity. Alcatraz is no exception. In fact, Alcatraz may be the most haunted prison in the world. The "Dungeon," which sits below the prison, is just one of many areas where spirits make themselves known, and it is part of the original citadel built as Fort Alcatraz. This area was used briefly as the isolation ward by the federal prison. Prisoners were routinely tortured here as punishment for breaking the rules of the prison. It is now accessible only by a door in the floor of A block.

A ranger working in the late afternoon once heard screams coming from the dungeons and, thinking it must be a tourist who had become lost from

Strip cell 14D is said to be the most haunted place on Alcatraz.

their group, hurried down the spiral staircase, following the screaming in what she called a "game of hide and seek." The ranger never found anyone. At the time this happened to her, she was a complete nonbeliever, but she was surprised when she found out her supervisor and fellow rangers had similar experiences with the cold and dark passageways of the dungeon.

Cell 14D, known as one of the "strip cells," has had so many things happen in it that it is hard to deny its haunted reputation. From the first report of a prisoner dying in the cell and then showing up in the inmate count the following morning, tales of a red-eyed demon and a violent former inmate have come almost daily from this isolation cell.

From Robert "the Birdman" Stroud playing checkers in his hospital cell, Al "Scarface" Capone playing his banjo in the showers and Alvin "Creepy" Karpis still working in the kitchens while humming the song from the Hamm's Beer commercial, Alcatraz has seen some of the most violent men in history hang around after their deaths. Others, such as those inmates who were killed during escape attempts and riots, like the "Battle of Alcatraz," may remain for fear that their living acts will send them somewhere worse than the Rock. Or maybe they are stuck at "Hellcatraz" for those same deeds. With strange tales of monsters, red-eyed demons, Sasquatch and sea serpents, along with an entire island infested with the ghosts of angry and vicious murderers and thieves, is it really that hard to admit that this tiny island in San Francisco Bay could be the most haunted place on Earth?

THE WINCHESTER HOUSE

The Winchester Mystery House is well known around the United States and the world. It is known for all of the oddities within its sprawling Victorian walls. It's perhaps the most haunted house in the country and is renowned for its matriarch, Sarah Winchester. But what, in reality, do we actually know about the home that was built by, as some say, a woman who was, at best, haunted by the ghosts of those killed by the rifle that made her one of the wealthiest women in the country or, at worst, insane? It might come as a surprise, but Sarah may have been neither; she may have simply been a private woman who loved amateur architecture and the charity she kept private and close to her heart rather than out in the open for the masses. Sarah, in her own right, was an enigma whose story may never come out into the open light of day.

Born Sarah Lockwood Pardee in 1839 or 1840 (sources differ) in New Haven, Connecticut, Sarah, with one brother and five sisters, grew up financially comfortable, if not wealthy. But her father, Leonard, having established himself as one of the finest finish carpenters in the area, made enough money and had enough influence to run in the upper circles of society. Pardee was also an abolitionist and freethinker, which helped shape Sarah into a person who cared deeply for others. Being influenced by her home life, Sarah became engrossed with educating herself and learned to speak four languages. She also became proficient in musical composition, as well as math and science. This quest for learning, along with her empathy for those in need, would play a big part in her life after she moved to the West Coast.

Historic American Buildings Survey, creator, and Sarah L. Winchester. East front. *Winchester House, 525 South Winchester Boulevard, San Jose, Santa Clara County, California, 1933; translated by Jandoli Lizmitter, documentation compiled after, photograph; Library of Congress, https://www.loc.gov/item/ca0959; photos from Survey HABS CA-2107.*

Because of her father's station, he was often invited to parties thrown by the elite of New Haven, and Sarah's father would often bring his wife and one of his daughters with him as a way to introduce them to the city's wealthy, eligible bachelors. Sarah, being a petite four feet, ten inches tall and weighing only ninety-five pounds, was considered a great beauty and garnered the nickname the "Belle of New Haven." Needless to say, those eligible bachelors would all gather around young Sarah whenever she came to one of the galas. It was at one of these parties that Sarah met the love of her life, William Wirt Winchester, and it wasn't long before he fell in love with her and the two married.

William Winchester was the son of one of the wealthiest families in Connecticut. His father, Oliver, left his shirt manufacturing company and invested in and took over the Volcanic Arms Company, eventually creating the Winchester Repeating Arms Company in 1866. Since Sarah and William ran in the same circles and were close in age, it is likely that they already knew each other before they "met" at one of the galas. But after the two fell in love, they were married in September 1862. About the same time that Oliver was creating the Winchester company, Sarah was giving birth to his granddaughter Annie. The Winchesters' young daughter became their life and joy, but almost immediately, the couple knew there was something ailing the child. No matter how many times they fed their daughter, she kept losing weight, until after only six months of life, Annie died from malnourishment. Unfortunately, Annie was born with a rare malady called marasmus, which is a protein disorder that keeps the body from processing calories and thus causes starvation no matter how much is eaten. The Winchesters would not have another child, and the death of Annie would haunt Sarah for the rest of her life.

By 1875, the Winchester Repeating Arms Company had become the largest rifle manufacturer in the country, due in no small part to the Winchester model 1873, which garnered the nickname the "gun that won the West." So popular was this rifle that Annie Oakley and Buffalo Bill Cody became famous for their prowess in using the gun in their exploits, and President Theodore Roosevelt put it to great use during his time before assuming office. Over 700,000 Winchester rifles were sold between 1873 and 1916, making it one of the most prolific rifle brands in history.

In December 1880, Oliver Winchester passed away, leaving his son William as head of the company. Unfortunately, William would not hold that title long, as he was already suffering from tuberculosis. Only three months later, in March 1881, William died from the disease, leaving his 50 percent majority share of the company to his wife. This death was the final straw for Sarah, who decided to move out to California, where two of her sisters lived with their husbands in the San Francisco Bay area. Her brother-in-law was the president of Mills College, and Sarah wanted to be around family. With her newfound wealth, she wanted to help take care of them, although they were doing just fine on their own. Before Sarah Winchester left New Haven—and because she had also inherited $20 million in cash—the now-widow left a large endowment to New Haven Yale Hospital for the study of the disease that killed her husband. This money was used to establish the Winchester Chest Clinic, which is still helping patients to this day.

In 1886, Sarah Winchester purchased an eight-room farmhouse on forty acres of land in the city of San Jose. After settling into her new life, Sarah began to imagine what type of home she would design. She started by hiring an architect to turn her dreams into a reality. Unfortunately, this architect—and the several others she fired—never seemed to be able to create the things that Sarah imagined. Sarah had always had an interest in architecture, and she decided that the best way to build her home was to design it herself. Aside from receiving $20 million when her husband died, she also received $1,000 a day (roughly $25,000 today), so money was no object. Sarah set out to renovate her property flush with new and radical ideas in design.

Since Sarah had no training in architecture, things did not always go as planned, and she constantly had to make changes when her ideas didn't pan out. In a letter to her sister-in-law, written in 1898, Sarah said, "I

Historic American Buildings Survey, creator, and Sarah L. Winchester. View looking west from the top floor. *Winchester House, 525 South Winchester Boulevard, San Jose, Santa Clara County, California, 1933; translated by Jandoli Lizmitter, documentation compiled after, photograph; Library of Congress, https://www.loc.gov/item/ca0959; photos from Survey HABS CA-2107.*

am constantly having to make an upheaval for some reason, for instance, my upper hall, which leads to the sleeping apartment was rendered so unexpectedly dark by a little addition that after a number of people had missed their footing on the stairs, I decided that safety demanded something be done." What that something was is still unknown. Regardless of the design mishaps, by 1895, the house had grown so large that it was gaining the attention of the media. The February 24, 1895 issue of the *San Francisco Chronicle*, as quoted by SFGATE, may have been the genesis of what the Winchester House has become today: "The sound of the hammer is never hushed…the reason for it is in Mrs. Winchester's belief that when the house is entirely finished, she will die." This is the first time continuous building was mentioned, but it would certainly not be the last. The article continued, "Whether she had discovered the secret of eternal youth and will live as long as building material, saws and hammers last, or is doomed to disappointment as great Ponce de Leon in his search for the fountain of life, is a question for time to solve."

During the devastating 1906 San Francisco earthquake, Llanada Villa (the official name given to the estate by Sarah Winchester) sustained significant damage. Upper rooms collapsed into the rooms below, chimneys collapsed and inner walls cracked and plaster fell. Sarah took it all in stride and continued on with the construction. In many cases, instead of demolishing and reconstructing, Sarah would simply have the builders bypass the damage and build over and around the ruined areas. This saved time and money, but it also caused great confusion. By the time Sarah passed away while living in one of her other homes, Llanada Villa had grown into a sprawling, confusing mansion, with 160 rooms, 47 fireplaces (but only 17 chimneys), 13 bathrooms, 47 staircases (a few that lead to dead ends), 2,000 doors, 9 kitchens, 52 skylights, more cupboards and closets than one can count and 10,000 windows. Was this a mansion designed and built by an insane, grieving woman or a woman running from the ghosts of her deadly company? Or is it simply something from the mind of an untrained, amateur architect who was out of her league but had too much money and time to spare?

So many stories have grown out of Sarah Winchester's life and the mansion she built in the once-rural area of San Jose that the truth of the matter has somehow gotten lost in the passage of time. One such tale that has grown out of the telling and retelling of the Winchester saga is the one that is now the most prominent and well known. It is related to the lives taken by Winchester rifles, Sarah's belief in spiritualism and her atonement for perceived wrongs, and it is also the catalyst for the extreme paranormal activity that occurs in the Winchester Mystery House today.

It has been said that after the death of her husband, Sarah Winchester sought out a well-known local psychic medium who told Sarah that a curse had been placed on her and her family by the spirits of those who had been killed by the Winchester rifle. In an act of revenge, this had been the cause of her daughter and husbands' deaths. The medium went on to say that the only way to keep the curse at bay was for her to move out west, buy a plot of land and continue to build a house, twenty-four hours a day, seven days a week, for the rest of her life. He told her that if the construction ever stopped, the spirits would enact their revenge and she would die. The research on this aspect of her life is fascinating, but due to space constraints, I will not go into it here. Suffice it to say, Sarah indeed moved out west, and these spirits are the catalysts for the ghosts of the ever-expanding mansion.

After Sarah Winchester passed away in 1922 and her estate settled, John H. Brown purchased the Llanada Villa. Brown had made a name for himself, along with a fair amount of money, designing and building roller coasters and creating amusement parks. After buying the mansion, John noticed that the reputation for the haunting of the house was true, and he began advertising the spirits of Llanada Villa. This caught the attention of Harry

Historic American Buildings Survey, creator, and Sarah L. Winchester. Sarah Winchester's bedroom, second floor. *Winchester House, 525 South Winchester Boulevard, San Jose, Santa Clara County, California, 1933; translated by Jandoli Lizmitter, documentation compiled after, photograph; Library of Congress, https://www.loc.gov/item/ca0959; photos from Survey HABS CA-2107*

Houdini, who decided to visit the mansion in 1924. The story goes that no matter how hard Houdini tried, he couldn't debunk the ghost stories, and he claimed that the house was a mystery to him. From that day on, Llanada Villa became known as the Winchester Mystery House.

The most famous spirit at the Winchester House is Clyde. This spirit is seen often, and you can tell it is Clyde by his overalls and cap. Clyde is often seen going about his duties in and around the home, which leads folks to believe he was a past caretaker of the property. According to the Winchester Mystery House's website, Clyde is also quite often seen by employees and guests pushing a wheelbarrow down in the basement of the mansion, and he is often seen busy at work in the ballroom, "repairing" the fireplace. There are times that guests claim Clyde sports a "handsome" mustache and wears a Victorian boater's hat.

Clyde seems to have a ghostly cohort who likes to remain unseen but is playful nonetheless. The website also talks about how guests and employees alike will feel gentle tugs on their shirts, long hair, skirts and other bits of clothing as they tour the mansion. It also relates a tale from one of the home's maintenance men who, one morning, heard the sound of footsteps above him as he entered the water tower. The employee ascended the three-story structure, following the footfalls, until he finally reached the roof. Once he was at the top, no one could be found. The Winchester House also states that psychics and mediums, many of them famous, have come to the mansion and picked up on Sarah Winchester herself. They said that Sarah expressed her happiness about having so many people visiting her home. It is nice to know that Sarah is happy in her afterlife.

In her book *Haunted San Jose* (The History Press, 2022), Elizabeth Kile not only wrote about Clyde but also says that the Winchester Mystery House has a lot of shadow figure activity. She also wrote about numerous reports of hearing laughter and people talking in empty rooms, doors opening and closing by themselves and doorknobs that turn with no visible hand operating them. One of the things that Kile mentions in her book is how folks often see an impression in Sarah Winchester's empty bed, as if someone is lying in it. The bed is in the room where Sarah lived, although it's not in the same location in the room. This figure is believed to be the spirit of Sarah Winchester herself. This room also has a personal history connection for me that may be related to this spectral figure in the bed, and this can possibly answer the question of who is lying there. Planet Paranormal visited the Winchester House back in 2015, and while we were standing outside Sarah's bedroom (it was roped off), my buddy Bob Davis tapped me on the shoulder, pointed to a spot on the floor and, there, in clear letters, were the scratches "SW." Bob and I figured that this was done by the staff and asked our tour guide about it. Our guide was confused and asked us to show her what we were talking about. When we returned to the spot, the letters were gone. However, the guide did tell us that spot was where Sarah had originally placed her bed when she lived in the house. Was this Sarah's way of telling us where she actually slept?

Kile also explained that a former manager of the mansion said that one evening, while closing up for the night, after all of the other employees and tour guides had gone home, he made sure that all of the lights were extinguished, set the alarms and headed out to his car. Before he set off, he glanced up at the house to make sure he hadn't forgotten any lights. He saw that all was dark and then headed for home. He went on to say that as he drove through the parking lot to the exit, he glanced up one more time and watched as all of the lights on the third floor began to turn on. One of the tour guides told Kile that once, while on the third floor, he heard footsteps near him but could not see anyone. Looking around, he noticed a figure out on the exterior of the house, only a few feet away from him. He said that as he approached the figure, it slowly disappeared. Many of the employees and tour guides say that the third floor is the most haunted area of the mansion, and many dislike having to go up there by themselves, especially late at night or early in the morning.

Many ghost stories about the Winchester Mystery House can be found online, but it can be difficult to distinguish truth from fiction. One story that has popped up says that a common sighting is that of a spirit that has

The famous "Door to Nowhere."

no name; it simply peers at folks while they tour the mansion. Some believe that it is a vengeful spirit left over from the days of the curse. I am leery of these types of stories in the light of TV shows and their "everything is 'demonic'" mentality. I have not been able to find any mention of a harmful spirit ever being witnessed at the mansion. On the contrary, most if not all the spirits appear to be playful or otherwise oblivious to the living. It would seem that many others, like their mistress, much prefer to remain by themselves, and while they are not reclusive, they are private with their afterlives.

Many folks claim that Sarah Winchester was a recluse, but after one learns about the life and history of this kind and generous woman, it becomes clear that she just enjoyed her privacy. Yes, she would attend parties, she would participate in fundraisers and social tête-à-têtes and she did have her own social circle, but she still relished her privacy at home and enjoyed time with her family above all else. In a time when the wealthy gave a lot to charity—as long as their good deeds were public—Sarah gave in private, never wanting adoration or admiration for her charitable deeds. For her, the giving was its own reward. This is the woman I came to know while writing this chapter.

Her death from heart failure in 1922 barely made the papers, with only a brief mention being made in the *Mill Valley Record*: "A few days ago, a quiet woman went quietly out of life, leaving a fortune of some millions, all of it for philanthropy." But Sarah's death brought forth a mystery that will never be solved and one that millions know about today. It will remain a mystery for as long as folks seek the strange and unusual. The Winchester Mystery House is a testament to one woman's determination to find perfection and remains a symbol of Sarah Winchester's desire to bring beauty and fascination to the people she truly cared about, the citizens of the United States.

Raz'n Hell at the Castle Air Museum

The Castle Air Museum affords visitors from around the region and throughout the world the opportunity to learn the costly sacrifices of the men and women who designed, built, maintained and flew these aircraft into hostile skies to defend freedom and liberty with many making the ultimate sacrifice.

These words from the museum's own website, along with its mission statement, "to preserve military aviation heritage for future generations," does not even begin to touch on the dedication of the museum's staff and volunteers who undertake the monumental task of restoring and preserving of historic aircraft. Some of them were left to the whims of the elements, and others needed so much work that they became jigsaw puzzles. The task of finding the pieces and fitting them together to re-create a complete, historically accurate aircraft is one lesser folks would have simply given up on. This was the case with the museum's B-29 heavy bomber, *Raz'n Hell*. Made from four different airplanes, *Raz'n Hell* certainly made the volunteers work for the reward, but it also refused to give up the ghost, at least the one the museum says haunts the B-29 and museum.

Originally opened on September 29, 1941, as the Army Air Corps Basic Flying School, Merced, Castle Airforce Base's mission was to train pilots and aircrew for the United States' growing bomber forces. The creation of the base came about when the army began looking for a suitable location to establish its training facilities. A group of Merced citizens got together after the army failed to consider Merced Airport and raised money to buy a plot

Castle Air Museum Gift Store.

of land that would accommodate the army's needs and offered to lease the land to the army for a dollar a year. So, on June 16, 1941, the U.S. Army Air Corps leased the land and began building the airfield the following July. It didn't take long to build a somewhat primitive base, with the airfield opening just two months later. In October, the army leased the previously passed-over Merced Airport as an auxiliary base.

At first, the trainees trickled in, but when the Japanese bombed Pearl Harbor on December 7, 1941, and the United States entered World War II, men began to enlist at a fevered pace. The call went out that the air corps was in need of pilots and crew, and recruits began flooding into the unfinished training base. The Merced auxiliary base became the main training base while the Army Air Corps Basic Flying School, Merced's field fought through severe rainy weather as its construction was completed. By the time the main base was finished, the name of the base had been changed to the Merced Army Flying School. This occurred on April 7, 1942, under the direction of the Western Flying Training Command, based at Moffett Field in Santa Clara, California. Some B-17 crews were trained at Merced Field, but its main focus was the newer, faster and more prolific B-24 Liberator bomber that was beginning to establish itself as America's premier heavy bomber. The B-24 may have been faster and could carry a heavier load than the Flying Fortress (B-17), but due to the new Davis Wing, the Liberator was much more difficult to fly. The Merced Army Flying School also had the distinction and honor of being one of the first bases to train WASPs (Women's Airforce Service Pilots).

Thousands of aircrews were trained at Merced Army Flying School during World War II, and with the end of the conflict, many air bases began to slow down or were shut down altogether, but not Merced Field. During the war, the aviation industry, at the behest of the Army Air Corps, began to develop air tankers for both air refueling and logistics. Many of these tankers were coming into service, and Merced Field became home to several tanker squadrons, as well as a training base for their pilots and crews. In 1946, the Merced Army Air Field was redesignated Castle Field in honor of a B-17 pilot who gave his life for his crew, earning him the Congressional Medal of Honor.

On December 24, 1944, Brigadier General Frederick W. Castle was leading two thousand B-17 heavy bombers of the Ninety-Fourth Bomb Group, Fourth Combat Wing. While en route to the target, General Castle's B-17 lost an engine, forcing him to drop out of formation to try to limp back to England. On the way back to base, his aircraft was attacked by a flight of German fighters. Usually, a damaged bomber that is being attacked by fighters would immediately jettison its bomb load to increase speed, but because Castle's B-17 was flying over Allied territory and he didn't know if there were friendly troops on the ground, Castle decided not to risk harming any friendlies on the ground. As the Luftwaffe fighters continued their attack on his stricken plane, the damage began to mount, and Castle ordered his crew to bail out. He knew that being over friendly territory, rather than over the English Channel, his crew had a very good chance of surviving to fight another day. Castle, wanting to make sure his crew was safe, stayed at the B-17's controls until the plane exploded from the massive amount of damage inflicted on it. All of the crew survived except for Castle and a crewman who had been killed before the bailout order. General Frederick Castle was posthumously awarded the Congressional Medal of Honor. The citation reads:

> *He was air commander and leader of more than 2,000 heavy bombers in a strike against German airfields on 24 December 1944. En route to the target, the failure of 1 engine forced him to relinquish his place at the head*

of the formation. In order not to endanger friendly troops on the ground below, he refused to jettison his bombs to gain speed maneuverability. His lagging, unescorted aircraft became the target of numerous enemy fighters which ripped the left wing with cannon shells, set the oxygen system afire, and wounded 2 members of the crew. Repeated attacks started fires in 2 engines, leaving the Flying Fortress in imminent danger of exploding. Realizing the hopelessness of the situation, the bail-out order was given. Without regard for his personal safety, he gallantly remained alone at the controls to afford all other crewmembers an opportunity to escape. Still another attack exploded gasoline tanks in the right wing, and the bomber plunged earthward, carrying Gen. Castle to his death. His intrepidity and willing sacrifice of his life to save members of the crew were in keeping with the highest traditions of the military service.

General Castle's other decorations include the Distinguished Service Cross, Legion of Merit, four Distinguished Flying Crosses, four Air Medals and the Purple Heart. On September 18, 1947, the U.S. Army Air Corps became the United States Air Force, and many of the old bases began to be renamed. So, it was on January 13, 1948, that the old Merced Field officially became Castle Air Force Base to honor a true American hero.

As new jet aircraft went into production, new bombers and transports found a home at Castle Air Force Base, C-54 transports and B-29 bombers, along with the improved model, the B-50, in 1949. Then in 1954, the six-engine, high-subsonic-speed B-47 Stratojet strategic bomber began arriving at Castle. Castle AFB became the training site for crews transitioning into the new jet aircraft. As such, when the Boing B-52 Stratofortress became available, training the crews for these behemoth heavy bombers (they could hold the equivalent of three railroad cars worth of fuel) fell squarely on the shoulders of Castle AFB. With the B-52s came the new KC-135 Stratotanker, which is still in use today.

The first nonstop, around-the-world flight of a jet aircraft (Operation Power Flight) began when three B-52s of the Ninety-Third Bombardment Wing took off from Castle AFB on January 16, 1957. After traveling 24,325 miles around the globe, they landed two days later at March AFB in Riverside, California. The flight was originally scheduled to land back where they had started, but it was diverted due to heavy fog obscuring the runways at Castle.

Castle Air Force Base continued to serve the United States over the intervening years, hosting President John F. Kennedy, taking first place in the annual SAC Bombing Competition in 1970 and sustaining its exemplary

Introduced in 1952, the giant B-52 bomber is still in use.

performance of training it had always been known for. No matter how proficient Castle AFB was, it couldn't escape Congress's cutting torch after the fall of the Berlin Wall. In 1990, the base was designated for closure under the Defense Base Closure and Realignment Act. The last B-52 left the base in 1994, with the KC-135 departing in early 1995. Castle Air Force Base closed for good on September 30, 1995. But this was not the end for the history and devotion of this great air base. In 1981, the Castle Air Museum, adjacent to the air base, now Castle Airport, opened to the public and keeps the spirit and valor of those who serve in the armed forces alive for future generations. It even has a haunted B-29 whose ghost wants to help in this endeavor.

Castle Air Museum has two Superfortress bombers in its amazing collection, and although these aircraft look very similar, they are actually two different aircraft. As Castle was one of the first bases on the West Coast to receive these warbirds, it is not surprising that the museum now has them as show pieces. One of these aircraft is actually a Boeing WB-50 Superfortress designated #49-0351. The B-50 was essentially a post–World War II updated B-29. The other, *Raz'n Hell*, is a standard B-29 that was common for bombing raids over Japan—well, maybe not completely standard. *Raz'n Hell* was enhanced with a large radar unit slung under its fuselage; it was this radar unit that gave the aircraft its name, R for "radar" and AZ for "azimuth." This is not the only thing that separates the two Superfortresses, however; *Raz'n Hell* also has Arthur, a ghost that helps the museum protect the old warbird.

Raz'n Hell is actually a composite B-29 made up of four different aircraft that were rotting in the California High Desert at China Lake Naval Station. For eighteen months, museum crew had to piece together parts from these four airplanes to create a historically accurate B-29 exterior. This was no easy task, as all of the pieces needed to be structurally sound and fitted together. It was during this time at China Lake that strange things began to happen around the museum crew. According to the museum, a crew member said that, in 1981, while still in the air force and stationed at Castle AFB, he had the opportunity to assist in the retrieval of *Raz'n Hell.* He said that while inside the craft, on his belly in a tight area, he reached around for his wrench and felt his partner hand it to him. After grabbing the wrench, he glanced out of a small porthole to see his partner across the way, taking a cigarette break. He was completely alone in the airplane and wondered whose hand he had felt passing him the tool. Other strange happenings were reported throughout the salvage operation at China Lake.

This was not the only incident that took place while museum crews prepared the B-29 for its journey to Castle Air Museum. While checking on the condition of the four bomb bay doors to make sure they would be ready for transport, the crews had difficulty getting one of the bays opened for inspection. The doors were not only rusted but also latched from the inside. Over the course of a couple of days, while trying to get the doors to move, the crew would leave the aircraft and then watch as the bay doors slowly opened and then shut again. Three times, this was witnessed, and three times, the crews rushed over to check the doors. But there seemed to be no change in the condition, and they still had to work a bit to get them to finally open. Tools would go missing and then turn up in another area of the fuselage, and odd tapping and banging was reported by the crew who were alone in the craft at the time. They said it sounded as if someone else was working inside with them. Could the spirit have been eager to have the airplane moved to a less-remote location and been trying to help hurry it along?

Once *Raz'n Hell* was ready for relocation to Castle Air Museum, the monumental task of getting it there became an issue. The fuselage could be transported by truck, but the wings, with a total wingspan of 141 feet, would need to be airlifted to the museum. The transport of the 99-foot-long main body of the B-29 went off without a hitch; the wings, however,

Raz'n Hell is perhaps the only bomber in history to be haunted by a former crewman.

were almost lost when, after being mounted on the helicopter incorrectly, they decided they wanted to "fly" on their own without the assistance of the heavy-lift chopper. This incident came close to causing the loss of not only the wings but also the helicopter. Luckily, the wings and the helicopter arrived at Castle AFB safely.

Once *Raz'n Hell* arrived at the museum, the work of putting it back together began. During this time, even more reports of ghostly encounters sprang forth from the restoration crews. More than twenty "strange occurrences" were reported to base security during the renovation process, and now, even the United States Air Force began to wonder whether the old B-29 was haunted. Before the final move to the museum, a volunteer snapped a picture inside the plane's fuselage, and when the film was developed, there, standing next to the aircraft's aft gun position, was a cloudy image that was quite discernable as a human figure. Now, with the rebuilding effort going full steam ahead, this figure was making itself known by becoming visible to the naked eye. Air force security had received a report of someone sitting in the cockpit of *Raz'n Hell* and promptly headed over to catch the intruder. Once they arrived at the old warbird, they spotted the person still sitting in the copilot's seat, but as they approached the bomber, they saw the figure disappear. Upon checking the interior of the B-29, they found that all of the hatches were secure, and no one was inside the airplane.

According to the museum itself, sometime in 1982, someone was driving past the AFB late one night when they noticed that the running lights were lit on *Raz'n Hell.* He knew some of the volunteers and was aware that they were in the process of getting power out to the old bomber, so he figured they had finally succeeded in their project. The next morning, the person drove to the museum to congratulate the volunteers, only to find out that the B-29 was still without power and that there was no way the running lights could have been shining.

After *Raz'n Hell* was completed and put on display, the reports of ghostly activity continued. This time, however, they came from the museum's visitors. Tales of the cockpit windows opening and closing on their own, sounds of knocking coming from the inside of the fuselage and figures moving around inside the unrestored bomber came up so often that a local news crew caught wind of them and wanted to do a report about *Raz'n Hell.* In 1993, this news team spent the night inside the old bomber. With cameras and microphones at the ready, they settled in to record anything strange that might happen. Almost immediately, unexplained incidences began to occur. At first, the walkie talkies began having strange interferences come through when the news crew tried to communicate with each other. Then their video equipment began to fail, with entire sections of tape being obscured and odd images of strange shadows and other things showing up and then disappearing at random. Then equipment, like the floodlights, simply began breaking and becoming unusable. Needless to say, the TV crew will never forget their night in the belly of *Raz'n Hell.*

With all of the high strangeness going on with the B-29, it was decided that an attempt would be made to find out who or what was causing all of the commotion. To this end, a séance was conducted inside *Raz'n Hell*, and those in attendance discovered that a former gunner by the name of Arthur was the spirit haunting the bomber. Unfortunately, they couldn't find out which of the four B-29s that were used to construct *Raz'n Hell* the crewman had flown with. However, Arthur being a gunner made sense, considering the figures that have been seen next to the aft gunner's position in various photos. Arthur seems intent on helping protect and refurbish the bomber, but it is unclear if he is also the ghost that sometimes haunts the museum's offices and building.

While I was interviewing the executive director of the museum, Joe Pruzzo, another longtime employee came into the office. After being introduced, he told us that he often comes in earlier than the other staff and can hear strange noises in some of the offices, but when he glances in, the noise immediately

The largest bomber to ever be used by America, the B-36 "Peacemaker" at the Castle Air Museum, is a wonder to behold.

stops. He went on to say that one night, while he was alone in the gift store, he felt a spirit walk right past him. One of the past museum superintendents, Master Sergeant Richard Zeunges, said that if Arthur truly exists, he felt that he "wanted to come in from the cold." He said that while closing the museum one winter night, he placed the office trash cans out in the hall so they could be dumped in the morning. Then he went downstairs to lock up the museum. While downstairs, he heard what sounded like one of the cans being moved. After running back upstairs to see if there was an intruder, he found that a bag from one of the cans had been taken out and placed next to the trash can. There was no one in the building other than Zeunges, and the doors were all locked.

Castle Air Museum is located in Atwater, California, and is the largest museum of its kind on the West Coast. With many of the aircraft still owned by the air force (those that came to the museum before the base's closure), taking care of the eighty-plus aircraft has challenges over and above those of other aviation museums. But the Castle Air Museum Foundation has never wavered in its responsibility of keeping the history of the air force, the aircraft and, as Arthur's spirit so eloquently can attest to, the men and women who dedicate their lives to keeping all of America safe.

The Santa Cruz Boardwalk

Is there anything better than a day at the beach? The sand squishing between your toes, your skin soaking up the warming rays of the sun and the cool ocean water easing away the stress of a long work week. Throw in a boardwalk with the sounds of children laughing, the smell of churros, hot dogs, deep-fried Twinkies, all mixed with the sweet aroma of a Pacific coast clambake, and you have the setting for a wonderful day with family and friends. But what if that ideal boardwalk is rife with spirits? Folks long dead and buried who still want to feel the thrill of the roller coasters, the suspense of the dark rides and the laughter of the funhouse mirrors? For most folks, this would be of only a passing interest in the light of day, but for the paratraveler, it makes for the perfect fun-filled adventure along the sunny California coast.

The Santa Cruz Boardwalk is the oldest amusement park and one of the last of its kind along the entire West Coast of the United States. Only two others remain in California: the Santa Monica Pier and Belmont Park in the Mission Beach area of San Diego. However, only Santa Cruz can trace its boardwalk beginnings to the 1800s. That is when John Leibrandt opened a public bathhouse at the mouth of San Lorenzo River. Folks flocked to the bathhouse, and soon, others arose nearby, until thousands of tourists came to soak in the "healing" natural salt water. Due to the influx of folks coming to the bathhouses, other tourist-related businesses, such as shops and restaurants, sprang up, and by the end of the century, the Santa Cruz beachfront was abuzz with activity. Enter Fred W. Swanton.

Entrance to the Boardwalk with the Double Shot ride in the background.

Born in Brooklyn, New York, in 1862, Fred and his family moved to California when he was only two years old. Growing up, Swanton heard tales of Coney Island from visiting friends and family, so he visited the boardwalk when he traveled to the East Coast and began dreaming about such a place out west. The Santa Cruz Boardwalk had its true beginnings when Fred Swanton opened his Neptune Casino, Plunge and Tent City resort near the bathhouses and tourist area in 1904. This fully electrified resort offered cottages and tents for guests to lay their heads while visiting the elaborate, Moorish-style casino that featured dance halls, restaurants, a stage for bands and a fully remodeled Plunge. To go along with his new resort, Swanton also installed an "electric" pier and carnival games. For two years, the resort saw guests enjoying the summers, but on June 22, 1906, it burned to the ground. The only things left standing were the roller rink, the pier and a few tents.

Swanton, who was elected mayor of Santa Cruz three times, was not the kind of man to cry over spilled milk, and he almost immediately began lining up financing to rebuild the casino. This time, however, Fred Swanton went even bigger than before and realized his dream of a Pacific Coast Coney Island. On June 15, 1907, just under a year after the fire consumed his old

Santa Cruz, California; Pillsbury Picture Co.; January 7, 1908. *DLC/PP-1908:43393, no. 3541.*

casino, the new casino rose from the ashes. This time, there was a grand ballroom, an indoor swimming pool, a new pleasure pier and a boardwalk to rival any on the East Coast. The boardwalk featured carnival games, food concessions and even a miniature railroad ride called the Bay Shore Limited. In 1908, the boardwalk's first thrill ride, known as the L.A. Thompson Scenic Railway, opened. This early, relatively tame roller coaster took riders along the shore on a fast-paced wooden track. But it was the Charles Looff hand-carved merry-go-round installed in 1911 that became—and still is—the Santa Cruz Boardwalk's pride and joy.

The boardwalk, almost from the beginning, became a favorite of families from all over the Bay Area, as well as tourists from out of state. It seemed as if Swanton had achieved his dream of a Pacific Coast Coney Island; however, one thing seemed to be missing. In the early 1920s, Looff's son Arthur convinced the board of the Santa Cruz Seaside Company (Swanton resigned in 1913) that the Scenic Railway should be replaced by a faster, more modern wooden roller coaster. The board agreed, and on May 17, 1924, the Giant Dipper opened to a waiting crowd. It didn't take long before the Dipper became the boardwalk's most popular ride, and it remains so to this day. Today, the Giant Dipper has carried more that 68 million riders along its track, reaching speeds of fifty-five miles per hour. The Giant Dipper roller coaster and the Looff Carousel, along with the original 1894 342-pipe Ruth band organ, have been recognized as National Historic Landmarks. Oddly enough, Belmont Park in San Diego also has its own Giant Dipper roller coaster. Although it's a year younger than the coaster in Santa Cruz, it was designed by the same noted coaster architects, Frank Prior and Frederick Church. The Giant Dippers are the last of the wooden coasters on the West Coast that were designed by these two, but the Belmont Shore's coaster is the only one whose construction was supervised by Prior and Church. The Dipper in San Diego is also listed in the National Register of Historic Places and has been designated a National Historic Landmark.

By 1934, the Casino Ballroom, still a centerpiece of the boardwalk, was seeing a decline, and a remodel was ordered. The Troyer brothers, who operated the boardwalk's Casa del Rey Hotel, redecorated the ballroom in a South Pacific theme, renamed it the Coconut Grove and ushered in new guests with some of the biggest names of the Big Band era. Then after World War II, the entire casino was "modernized" (many were upset at the new look of the building), and the casino and Coconut Grove are still going strong to this day. After Disneyland came on the scene and reimagined what an amusement park could be, thoughts turned to new ride ideas, and 1961 ushered in a new era for the Santa Cruz Boardwalk.

In 1956, the boardwalk's east end was expanded between the Giant Dipper and the river mouth. An 825-foot-long concrete wall was put in place with a new "deck" on top. This allowed for more ride space on the upper deck, with maintenance shops, storage and public restrooms located in the basement area. Then after Walt Disney built his park and created the "theme park," guests at all other amusement parks began to expect the same innovations. So, in July 1959, the boardwalk began constructing two new rides to fulfill the expectations of its visitors. One of these was similar to a mine train attraction and was called the Cave Train to the Lost World. Where Disneyland had both a mine train ride and another train that took guests past the Jurassic era, the Cave Train to the Lost World combined the two themes into one ride. Through darkened caves, guests could view amusing cave dwellers in their "normal" habitats and ride past menacing dinosaurs. The ride was a huge success. Today, the ride remains as Cave Train 2000, with renovations and upgrades aplenty.

The other ride also came about because of Disney and its Autopia ride. As popular as this ride was, once the Federal Highway Act passed and America took to the roads, kids who were too young to drive flocked to Disney's Fantasyland Autopia, and the board of the Santa Cruz Boardwalk took notice. Having a brand-new deck above what would become the Cave Train, the Santa Cruz Autorama was built and became an instant success when it opened in June 1961. By 1963, the boardwalk's Autorama ride was so well known that Walt Disney himself visited the boardwalk to see what all the fuss was about. Walt drove one of the cars, discussed the safety of the center guide rail configuration (Autopia had no rail, just a curbed track), signed a few autographs for boardwalk guests and left. Within two years, Walt Disney had changed his Autopia ride to include a center guide rail and

The entrance to Neptune's Kingdom in Santa Cruz, the county seat and the largest city in Santa Cruz County, California. *The Jon B. Lovelace Collection of California Photographs in Carol M. Highsmith's America Project, Library of Congress, Prints and Photographs Division.*

removed the concrete curbs. Unlike the Cave Train to the Lost World, the Autorama (renamed The Great Auto Race) was removed in 1998, as the new master plan for the boardwalk called for more rides and the only area where they could fit was the upper deck where the Autorama was located. The ride may be gone, but so many folks have fond memories of the Autorama that it will never be lost.

Today, the Santa Cruz Boardwalk is still a popular tourist destination, and it has grown to include more than forty rides and attractions, twenty-two midway games, more than forty food stands, numerous gift stores, four video arcades with hundreds of games and even an electronic shooting gallery. The Coconut Grove is still going strong, and there is even a Southern Pacific passenger train that takes guests to the nearby town of Felton and back four times a day; it stops directly in front of the boardwalk. This famous location has one other thing to offer: plenty of ghosts up and down the entire stretch of the beach.

Maybe it is because of the crowds, the gaiety that is ever present on the boardwalk or the fact that there have been so many folks who have spent time here with their family and friends, but the Santa Cruz Boardwalk has more than its fair share of spirits that haunt its environs. Luckily, employees who work at the boardwalk were not scared or reluctant to speak with me about the happenings at the amusement park.

The casino was the beginning of the boardwalk, and even though it has changed a few times throughout its history, there seem to be a few folks from its long past who have decided it is a great place to spend their afterlife. The activity within this historic building is mild, but over the years, those working in the casino have heard phantom footsteps and the sounds of parties being held in the ballrooms, even when they are completely empty. Many times, staff have reported the sound of laughter, music and conversation within the empty halls and rooms of the casino. Even after all this time, it seems that the good times still roll in the boardwalk casino.

Close to the casino on the boardwalk proper is the old arcade building. Here, employees have told stories of hearing the sounds of kids laughing and playing long after the building is closed. There was one report about the machines coming to life in the early morning hours, as if a large group of kids was playing the games. But even as security watched the games being played, no one could be seen manipulating the buttons. As the guards walked by each machine, the games stopped, turned off and remained dark for the rest of the early morning. There is another place within the arcade that has so many reports of paranormal activity that few can deny it is happening; that place is the laser tag attraction. Here, many stories have been told about

Once a public pool, Neptune's Kingdom is now a haunted shopping and miniature golf venue.

a man and a little kid who are seen wandering around inside the laser tag arena. It is said that they are dressed in "old-style" clothes, with the man wearing a suit and, on occasion, a bowler hat. The spirits have been seen on both levels of the game arena, and on occasion, their shadows have caused those playing the game to "give up" their hiding places and be "shot" by the opposing team. I was told that there is a little girl who is seen within the laser tag arena, running around and looking as if she wants to play with the other gamers. This girl is not wearing one of the laser tag backpacks, but she seems to be having the time of her life. I am a bit confused about this spirit, as no one could tell me if this is the same child that appears with the suited gentleman previously mentioned.

Double Shot is a 125-foot-tall thrill ride on the boardwalk near the arcade, where riders sit in an open seat as they are catapulted to the top of a tower, dropped and then shot back up in a stomach-churning adventure that is guaranteed to make them smile and scream. This ride, along with all of the others, closes when the park shuts down, but unlike other attractions, Double Shot seems to keep going long after everyone has gone home for the evening. Employees at the boardwalk have told me that in the middle of the night, the ride will suddenly come to life and begin to operate, even though there is no one at the controls. The car will seem to wait as if it is being loaded with riders and will then shoot skyward, drop and repeat before it seemingly waits to let the phantom riders off and then load another group of thrill seekers. This will happen only a couple of times, and then the ride once again remains quiet for the night.

One of the most haunted places on the Santa Cruz Boardwalk is Neptune's Kingdom. This building is where the original natatorium (Plunge) was located from 1907 until 1963, when it was finally shut down; now, the building houses a miniature golf course, a pool hall, air hockey and pinball machines, shops and a restaurant. But just because the swimming pool is gone, that doesn't mean those who once enjoyed the natatorium gave up the ghost after death claimed them. As happens when pools and revelry come together, accidents happen and, unfortunately, people drown. Over the many decades the Plunge was open, this happened more than we want to think about. One of those who drowned was a little girl who, it would seem, has stayed long after she left behind her mortal remains. This child has been seen and heard on the second floor of Neptune's Kingdom, running and playing, still in her bathing suit. There have also been numerous times that folks have heard a little girl's laughter while on the miniature golf course (this is where the pool was located before it was converted to its current use).

Security has reported hearing the sounds of water splashing in the middle of the night, long after the building has closed, and many wonder if there is more than just the little girl still enjoying the warm pool that is no longer there. These same security guards have said that they do not like going up to the third floor of the building, as they've repeatedly heard the sound of footsteps following them. Many no longer turn to see who is behind them because they know they will not see anyone, and many say that they are afraid of what they might see.

It is not only the upper floors where strange things are heard, as one of the employees told me that he routinely hears phantom voices in the maintenance tunnels when there is nobody there. There also seems to be strange things afoot in the shops that fill the lower floor of Neptune's Kingdom. Speaking with some of the shop clerks, it's clear that it is not uncommon for things to move about the shops on their own and for things to simply fall off shelves for no apparent reason. The Magic Shop has the same occurrences as the other stores; however, I was told that things became much worse when the owner brought in a Ouija board–patterned mouse pad for the shop's computer. Once the new pad was in use, things ramped up in the shop. So many things fell and jumped off the shelves that the mouse pad had to be removed. Once it was gone, things went back to their normal paranormal happenings.

After the east end of the boardwalk was expanded, the basement area added one of the new rides, Ghost Blasters, which still exists today and is still thrilling riders and ghosts alike. The basement is known for having a fair amount of paranormal activity, and it is said that many of these occurrences take place within the Ghost Blasters ride. Guests and employees alike have reported seeing figures that are obviously not a part of the ride, and a few have been so startled that they said they would never ride Ghost Blasters again. It is said that these spirits are also seen in the employee-only areas, where the phantoms will simply watch the employees and then vanish from sight.

The Giant Dipper roller coaster is by far the most popular ride at the Santa Cruz Boardwalk. Coaster enthusiasts come from all over the world to ride this historic wooden coaster, just to mark it off their bucket list. What many don't know is that it may be one of the most haunted roller coasters in the country—and the world. Not one person I talked to at the boardwalk failed to mention the ghost of the Giant Dipper. There were a few deaths in the early days of this wooden wonder, but it seems that one individual has remained behind to wish riders fun as they set off on their thrilling

This roller coaster comes with its own phantom ambassador.

adventure. No one is sure who the gentleman ghost is, but he has been seen so many times that no one denies his existence. This spirit is mostly seen at the top of the first drop, where he smiles and waves at the riders as they pass by to begin their adventure. He is seen at all hours of the day and night and has even been seen after closing and before opening, as if he is inspecting the rails and structure to make sure all is well. The man is said to be dressed in "old-style" clothes, so all we are certain of is that he is from an earlier time in the boardwalk's history. So, if you are riding the Giant Dipper and see this spirit, return his smile, wave and enjoy the ride.

The Santa Cruz Boardwalk is one of those places that is timeless in its family values of fun and entertainment. From its humble beginnings in the late 1800s, through the 1900s and right on into the new century, this beachfront pleasure zone has withstood time and remains a destination for vacationers from around the world. It also seems to be a destination for many spirits that have remained in the afterlife to continue enjoying the sunshine, beach, corndogs and all that the Santa Cruz Boardwalk has to offer.

Fort Ord

When one thinks about military bases, the word *beauty* is usually the last thing that comes to mind. However, Fort Ord, located along the Monterey Bay, may be the exception to this rule. Since its inception in 1917, this army base was considered one of the most sought-after posts where a soldier could be stationed. Here, troops trained under a canopy of trees on chaparral plains and along the pristine beaches of the Pacific Ocean. During their off time, troops could sun themselves along these same beaches while hanging out with local girls, visit the towns of Seaside or Monterey to enjoy local cuisine and fresh seafood or head up to San Francisco to revel in the city's famous nightlife. Even through World Wars I and II, Fort Ord was the base to be. But as great as things were for the many troops who trained and manned the base, there were things hidden underneath the surface that would eventually make the base shut its gates for good and bring an environmental scare to the entire Monterey Bay area that still rears its ugly head today. Not to mention the spirits that still lurk in the shadows of the base and its remaining buildings.

In 1916, as World War I raged in Europe, Congress passed the National Defense Act of 1916. This act authorized the U.S. Army to build up its artillery corps to include twenty-one field artillery regiments. By 1917, when the United States officially entered the war, these units had eight thousand officers and men. Training these regiments required huge parcels of land to set up artillery ranges, and to this end, the army purchased 15,809 acres of land in the Monterey Bay area from David Jacks, a local rancher. This area became known as the Gigling Reservation (East Garrison). The Gigling

Historic American Buildings Survey, creator, Savo Milan Stoshitch, Orville Pierce, William Henry Rowe, Joseph W. Stilwell, Winifred Alison Smith Stilwell, Alison Stilwell Cameron, et al. Fort Ord, Soldiers' Club, California State Highway 1, near Eighth Street, Seaside, Monterey County, California, 1933. *Martin Stupich, photographer; translated by Maul Davidmitter; documentation compiled after, photograph; Library of Congress, https://www.loc.gov/item/ca2607.*

family were German immigrants who had a dairy farm on the land. The first units to arrive and use the new reservation were those of the horse-drawn Seventy-Sixth Field Artillery, known as the "Black Horse" Regiment, who were stationed at the Presidio of Monterey, and the Thirtieth Infantry Regiment stationed in San Francisco. Both of these units used the East Garrison for maneuvers.

More and more units, mostly reserve and national guard units, came to what, at that time, was known by various names—Gigling Reservation, United States Field Artillery Range Presidio of Monterey, Camp Gigling or Gigling Field Artillery Range—to train. Then in 1919, Cavalry Commander John Jenkins set up his headquarters at the Presidio of Monterey, and the Eleventh Cavalry arrived to make Camp Gigling their home. By 1933, the army had decided that a permanent name was required to replace the many different names the camp had become known by, so Gigling Reservation officially became known as Camp Ord in honor of Major General Edward Otho Crespin Ord. As a lieutenant commanding Company F, Third Artillery, Ord had established the Presidio of Monterey on January 28, 1847.

Not much had been done at Camp Ord over the years, with very little construction taking place other than the inclusion of a rough dirt road that connected the East Garrison to a railway spur at Highway 1 (Pacific Coast Highway). Since the camp was used mostly as a field artillery range for the Seventy-Sixth Field Artillery and maneuver range for the Eleventh Cavalry and Thirtieth Infantry, it was deemed unnecessary to add improvements. That all changed as the specter of war grew with Italy's invasion of Ethiopia, Japan's invasion of China and Hitler's demands and threats in Europe. In

1938, the commanding officer of the Presidio of Monterey, Colonel Homer Groninger, appropriated $800,000 and, working with the WPA (Works Progress Administration), built a large camp about a mile away from the railroad spur. He also cleared a large section of brush and vegetation for future development. This was the beginning of one of the largest camps in U.S. history.

In July 1940, General Joseph "Vinegar Joe" Stilwell took command of the newly reformed Seventh Infantry Division (ID), and Stilwell was the driving force behind the now-famous million-dollar Soldiers Club that stood in what is now Fort Ord Dunes State Park and began building the mess halls, barracks and tents in the East Garrison for his newly arrived troops. Then, knowing that the war would require thousands of troops to be trained all around the country, more land was acquired, bringing the total land area to 29,610 acres. Camp Ord was now the size of the city of San Francisco and was redesignated as Fort Ord. After the attack on Pearl Harbor, Fort Ord saw a huge influx of personnel pass through, and Ord became one of the main training bases for troops being deployed overseas. Most of the troops were deployed to the PTO (Pacific Theater of Operations). Fort Ord was also the staging area for the Seventh ID to undergo amphibious training in 1943 before they were deployed to the Aleutian Islands. At any given time, there was an average troop concentration of thirty-five thousand at Fort Ord; however, at its peak, fifty thousand troops were trained here every year. For many soldiers, their last memory of the United States was of the Monterey area.

Once the war was over, Fort Ord became one of the primary "repatriation" centers for veterans returning to civilian life. Many of the men who had passed through Fort Ord on their way to battlefields of the PTO now found themselves coming back through and heading for home. In 1947, the Fourth Infantry Division was reactivated to begin training the army's replacements. Fort Ord was now home to the Fourth Replacement Training Center. This continued until September 1950, when the Fourth ID was transferred to Fort Benning, Georgia, while the Sixth ID assumed training duties at Fort Ord. Many of those who trained at Fort Ord during this time found themselves in the Korean Conflict. Fort Ord continued to be one of the main training centers for the U.S. Army through Korea, Viet Nam and on into the 1970s. Stationed at the Fritzsche Army Airfield (named in honor of Major General Carl Fritzsche) were the Fifty-Second Aviation Battalion, the Seventeenth Aviation Company and the Thirty-Third Transportation Company (Light Helicopter). Other units were engineer battalions, signal corps and ordnance.

In the early 1980s, the Seventh Infantry Division was reactivated at Fort Ord to establish the new "Light" Infantry Divisional theory. The Seventh ID would remain at Fort Ord until the base's closure in 1994. Today, the Seventh ID is stationed at Joint Base Lewis-McChord in Washington State and is the only active-duty multicomponent division headquarters (units that mix active duty and reserve personnel) in the U.S. Army. The reason the Seventh ID was transferred to Washington State was because the Base Closure and Realignment Commission recommended that Fort Ord be closed permanently. So, in September 1994, Fort Ord shut its gates and became the largest military base to date to be shut down.

Although the army retained about 785 acres, it was unclear what to do with the rest of the property. The neighboring communities of Seaside and Marina received large areas of the land bordering their cities, while Monterey acquired only a sliver of the old fort's land. Another large area was set aside and given to the California State University System for use as its new California State University, Monterey Bay. Much of this land had significant importance due to the many historical structures that were within it. Unfortunately, the only building that was officially designated as a historic structure was Stilwell Hall (Soldiers Club). Donated land or not, the municipalities could not decide how they wanted to use the land, with ideas ranging from golf courses and shopping malls to amusement parks and artist colonies. With the various cities unable to come to agreement, the State of California finally stepped in and made the decisions for them. Some of the land was given over to the state and became Fort Ord Dunes State Park, and 14,651 acres were set aside as the Fort Ord National Monument in 2012 by President Barack Obama. This area is under the jurisdiction of the Bureau of Land Management and is considered a wildlife habitat and sanctuary.

As mentioned, other than Stilwell Hall, nothing else was deemed "historical"; however, as institutes of higher learning are considered stewards and keepers of history, one would think that the university would be a careful guardian of our country's past. In California, at least, this is not always true, especially where the U.S. military is concerned. It is understandable that many of the structures within the new school grounds would need to go, but others should have been recognized for their historical significance. However, in 2008, the president of California State University, Monterey Bay, Dr. Dianne Harrison, said, "One of our ongoing frustrations—at least, it's mine—is all of those old, empty barracks and other buildings and unidentifiable things. I honestly don't know what they are. If only we

Ghosts still reside in the decaying barracks of Fort Ord.

could afford to take them all down today, I would be a very happy person." Unfortunately, she decided that she was going to make herself happy by destroying the last building of its kind within the United States, historically significant or not.

One of the first units to arrive at Fort Ord in 1917 was the horse-drawn Seventy-Sixth Field Artillery Regiment, and then in 1919, the Eleventh Cavalry was stationed at Fort Ord. Other cavalry units trained at the camp until the nation's cavalry units became mechanized. With so many units coming to train at the camp, Fort Ord became one of the largest cavalry bases in the United States. As such, facilities for the care and housing of the horses were needed, as were blacksmith and veterinary support. All of this was provided for not only the Eleventh Cavalry, who called Fort Ord their home, but also the visiting units who trained here. These facilities survived all the subsequent wars and were still intact at the time Fort Ord was closed. They did not, however, survive Dr. Harrison.

Harrison, who later tried to justify her earlier comments, said that because none of the buildings were identified as historical and she was afraid students would enter the structures and find scavengers and wildlife, they needed to go. In their place, she said, "I think building something really respectful which honors the tradition of where CSUMB started and what used to be here would be fabulous." She went on to say that her chief of staff told her that the stables were hardly ever used for horses and were converted to truck facilities in 1938. Where her subordinate got this information is unknown, but it certainly wasn't from any army historians. According to U.S. Army Veterinary Corps researcher Greg Krenzelok, the stables housed more than 1,400 army horses until 1942, and there is no proof they were ever used for another purpose. Even after the cavalry was mechanized, the fort kept a large horse presence until 1944.

For two years, Krenzelok fought to keep the stables and blacksmith buildings from being torn down. Then in May 2011, while Krenzelok was on assignment in Alaska, CSUMB demolished the "last complete example of our country's end of the U.S. Warhorse which were still being used at the beginning of World War II." Krenzelok went on to say that "artillery, cavalry stables along with their blacksmith shops were demolished on the California State University at Monterey Bay Campus, California. Leaving only the Veterinary Horse Hospital, the only building to testify of the memory of the 'Fort Ord Horse Soldiers.'...President Diane Harrison, who I personally hold responsible for this action and university's failure or interest to recognize the historical significance is one of the greatest tragedies to fall upon this university....The 'Honoring' of the history of Fort Ord has not been served by this action."

California has become well known for despising anything of a military nature, and it is not uncommon for cities and institutions, especially so-called places of higher learning, to try to get rid of anything they deem part of the "military industrial complex," regardless of the historical significance of what they are destroying. Unfortunately, it would seem that history is not high on the list of things needed to be taught—or kept—to achieve this higher learning. This destruction of the fort and its history may be one of the reasons that so many of the soldiers, military family members, officers and others have remained or come back after death. Old Fort Ord has now garnered a reputation for being one of—if not the most—haunted locations in all of Northern California.

It is well known that many old military bases around the world are haunted. No one really knows the truth behind the haunts, but folks surmise that it is mostly related to the deaths involved with the job. Training accidents, mistakes during maneuvers, unknown deadly medical conditions brought to the fore during the rigors of military duty and mental stress and illness that can cause one to lose hope and commit the ultimate act of suicide, all of these factors can be and are found on military bases everywhere. So, it really should come as no surprise that Fort Ord, being one of the largest bases in the United States, would have its fair share of ghostly activity.

It is not hard to find stories about the spirits of Fort Ord online. There are internet forums, such as Reddit, where folks talk about "the creepiest place in Monterey Bay," and there are websites devoted to military ghosts around the world. At Fort Ord, it is well known that things get strange when the coastal fog wafts through the base. One story that I heard was not a big surprise, because I had heard the same tales about other bases as well, even the military cemetery where my folks are buried in San Diego (*Haunted Heart of San Diego*, The History Press). Folks who've walked around the base and on the hiking trails of the nature preserve have reported that when the fog rolls in at dusk, strange sounds can be heard within the fog itself. Many are not sure if these sounds are simply hidden by the fog or come from the fog itself. These same people say that the creepiness is amplified by the fact that the fog also seems to absorb the natural sounds around them. Even their own voices sound hollow when they speak. Many of the local hikers and explorers, upon seeing fog come in from the coast, hurry to leave the area before it envelops them and the base in its mist.

One of the most-told stories regarding the spirits at Fort Ord is about a soldier who supposedly died by suicide in one of the barracks. This story is so well known that it can be found in the University of California's Digital Folklore Archives. It seems that a soldier who was stationed here may have been mentally ill and suffering from schizophrenia or some other mental illness (some say he went crazy because he kept seeing the ghosts that haunted his barracks). He became so distraught that one night, he hanged himself in front of his squad (it is unclear if any of his buddies tried to stop him). It is said that after his body was removed from the barracks, strange things began to happen there. The night after the man's death, the soldiers began hearing the sound of phantom footsteps walking between the cots, stopping momentarily and then walking away down the main aisle, only to stop at the next man sleeping. This continued until the barracks were abandoned after the base closed. Many folks and urban explorers have reported being in the abandoned barracks and hearing these same footfalls, even long after Fort Ord was closed. As I cannot find any reference to the year this death by suicide occurred or any confirmation on which barracks this soldier resided in, it is possible this may simply be an urban legend; however, I will leave it to my readers to decide on the validity of this tale.

The previous story, as I mentioned, is one of the most widely told tales regarding the hauntings of Fort Ord. It is also one of the tales mentioned in

Graffiti now replaces the once spit-and-polished army barracks.

the podcast *Spirits & Cousins with Tish and Courtney* (season 1, episode 6, June 26, 2023, "The Fort Ord Investigation"). I have listened to this podcast quite a bit and have found it to be not only a wealth of information about the paranormal activity around the Monterey Bay and Northern California but also a great way to learn about the location's history (all paratravelers should certainly check this podcast out). During the hosts' investigation of Fort Ord, they had some amazing things happen to them.

The show begins with the cousins talking about the many reports they have heard from locals in the area. Stories about hearing disembodied voices, footsteps and other strange sounds in and around the barracks. Folks will not only hear spirits walking around in the National Monument area of Fort Ord, but they will also see spirits wandering around at night and see shadows out of the corners of their eyes. On occasion, they will actually see full-bodied apparitions. Much of the national monument was part of the training area of the base, so it makes me wonder if these phantoms were soldiers who were killed in accidents or if they are still hanging out because of a sense of duty.

The hosts mention not only the legend of the suicidal soldier but also a couple of other tales they discovered from other folks. One of these tales was from someone who had actually lived on the first floor of one of the barracks. This person told them that they kept hearing 1940s music coming from under their bed. Every time he would hear the music, he would look under the bed, expecting to find a radio, recorder or other device, but he never found anything that could have been playing the music. He was sure that one of his buddies was playing a joke on him, that is until one evening when he was woken by a voice telling him, "There is someone at the door." Sitting up, he realized he was alone in the barracks, and then the front door opened and a group of his friends walked in, all of them drunk and laughing. It was then that he began to believe something else was going on in his barracks.

The hosts also talk about a woman who lived at the base, beginning when she was one year old. She remembers her mother putting her in a playpen with her toys and her favorite book, which was very large. She went on to say that she could remember this book moving across the playpen by itself on occasion, as if someone was moving it. She also said that as she grew older, their cat would suddenly get up, walk over to the bedroom and just stare into the room as if it was keeping an eye on someone. When she was older and in her room, she would hear her mother calling her to tell her to get off her phone. The odd thing about these times was the fact that neither she nor her mother was on the phone, yet she heard her mother's voice sounding as though she was on a call. The garage in their apartment building was also "creepy," and they came to believe that it was also haunted, as they would always get a strange feeling whenever they were there. Military personnel who came over to visit and others who lived there would always salute the garage before heading into the apartment. They never did receive an explanation for this.

So many things happened while they were living in the apartment building that they ended up calling in a paranormal team to try to get some answers about what was going on. The team set up remote cameras and listening devices, and during their investigation, they recorded an EVP (electronic voice phenomenon) that identified the ghost as a Major Redmon. Later, after some research was done, they found that there was never a Major Redmon stationed at Fort Ord; however, they did find a Major Hartman who had passed away on the base. This would explain the military personnel's salutes as they passed the garage (there was no information of Major Hartman passing away in or near the apartment). The former resident said that after these salutes, the activity in the garage would calm down for a while before slowly picking up again. Another EVP the paranormal team captured during their investigation—and one that they believe was directed to the mother—was a voice saying, "Your baby can hear me."

The hosts of *Spirits & Cousins* also had their own ghost stories to tell from their time investigating Fort Ord. They say that when they were in the barracks directly across from the old base chapel, trying to communicate, a clear "hi" came across their device. After asking a few direct questions, the women discovered the name of the person they were talking to: Daniel. After trying to coax more information out of Daniel, the women decided to head out for another location. As they left the barracks, one of the oddest things that ever happened to them occurred. Looking up the road, they saw headlights speeding toward them. Thinking it was either security or the police, they rushed to their own vehicle, but the other car was coming so fast that before they could get into their own car, the other was upon them. When the other car was only about ten yards away, it took a high-speed tight turn right into the tiny parking lot of the chapel. This parking lot could fit perhaps only five or six cars and was only twenty feet deep, but the speeding vehicle didn't even bother to put its brakes on as it turned. The hosts say they watched as the car sped through and past the parking lot into "dirt and scrub bushes." They go on to say that the car "flew into blackness, through the dirt, never to be seen again." They say that the odd thing about this car was that as it sped past and down into the lot and empty dirt field, no dust was ever kicked up; they got a good look at the car as it flew past them and said that it was "an older car." Running over to the parking lot, the women looked out into the wilderness, but even though only a few seconds had passed, they could see no head or taillights anywhere in sight. What they did notice, however, were the narrow posts that blocked cars from inadvertently driving off into the scrub.

As strange as this incident was, the women were not deterred from their investigation and headed over to the officers' housing area. Unlike the enlisted personnel, the officers had their own houses, albeit small, that were certainly more comfortable than the barracks. These officers' quarters were also segregated from the main base. Here, the hosts made contact with a spirit by the name of Charlie. Even though they were using several devices, it would seem that Charlie was a bit shy and didn't want to speak on a recorder. Instead, he preferred to use the "flashlight" method of communication. This is where a mini Maglite is barely turned on (contact is so light that the flashlight is actually off) and the spirit makes the light blink on, once for yes and twice for no (or ghosts hunters' choice). This was the method used to determine Charlie's name. The women used the alphabet, and when they reached the letter C, the light blinked "yes." From there, names beginning with C were called out until the light blinked "yes" again. Using this method, they found out that even though Charlie was still hanging around the base, he wasn't actually stuck there. They found out that Charlie was in the army, although there was no mention of whether he had been an officer, NCO (noncommissioned officer) or simply an enlisted man who liked the officers' quarters. It turns out that Charlie loved the area so much that he decided to come back to the area after he left the service and remained there until he passed. Charlie went on to say that he comes and goes through the veil when he chooses.

One more thing that the show's hosts mentioned happened just after they left the house where they made contact with Charlie. Since they were investigating on a very cold night, before heading home, they went to their car to warm up a bit. During the time they were sitting there, Courtney looked over at Tish and asked her if the rear windows were open. Tish told her no, they were both up, and then asked why she had asked. Courtney told her that she had just felt a cold "gust of wind or someone blowing down my neck," which gave her a huge chill that ran down her body. This was enough excitement for both women, who headed home with some amazing experiences.

Both Tish and Courtney say they never felt threatened or frighted by any of the spirits they encountered at Fort Ord and will most certainly return for another investigation (and, we hope, another episode of *Spirits & Cousins*).

When Fort Ord was closed down, the cities of Seaside and Marina suffered a huge economic loss. In total, twenty-one thousand jobs were

Once the pride of the U.S. Army, what remains at Fort Ord isn't even a shadow of its former glory.

lost, five thousand homes and apartments were vacated and $400 million in payroll checks and service contracts were lost. The two cities are making a comeback, but it will never be the same without the tens of thousands of army personnel stimulating the local economy. The tourist trade of Monterey Bay is a big help, and with the hotels in Marina and Seaside being much less expensive than those in Monterey proper, I highly recommend any paratraveler thinking about visiting the haunted locations in the area to look into to these communities. As I mentioned, Fort Ord has a reputation for being very haunted, and after the stories I found and listening to *Spirits & Cousins: With Tish and Courtney* (again, I highly recommend it), it is understandable why it has garnered this reputation. So, for all of my intrepid readers and paratravelers, head on up to Fort Ord to have a hauntingly good time.

CANNERY ROW

It's hard to think about Monterey, California, without Cannery Row springing to mind. From the Monterey Bay Aquarium anchoring one end of the road to an old, beat-up cannery claiming the other, folks from around the world come to this tourist mecca for all kinds of entertainments. Shops, restaurants, boutiques and the usual touristy sundries can all be found on Cannery Row. There was even a great magic shop that was located right next to the bust of John Steinbeck, which sits proudly at the entrance to Steinbeck Plaza. Not only did this shop sell fun and amazing magic supplies, but the owner also provided a fun and unusual Ghost Walk of Cannery Row, which you can still attend to this day. Yes, this tourist mecca is actually haunted. That should come as no surprise when one realizes that this area began with the blood, sweat and tears of workers canning millions of smelly fish, caught by hundreds of hardworking fishermen, simply trying to survive any way they could.

This area of Monterey was first inhabited by the Ohlone tribe of Natives, who grew food in the fertile soil and gathered fish as their main protein source. Later, the Spanish arrived and found the area so well suited to homesteading that they made Monterey the capital of Alta California. After a while, especially after the United States gained control of California, immigrants began arriving to the area, settling along the shore and fishing the abundant waters of the Monterey Bay. The Chinese were the first large ethnic group to settle the area, arriving in large numbers from China and taking up residence at Point Ohlones, later referred to as "China Point." It was this group who would establish the fishing industry in Monterey.

Historic American Engineering Record, creator, Knute Hovden, Stanford University, Wilbur Ellis Company, Pietro "Pete" Ferrante and William Lunde. Hovden Cannery, 886 Cannery Row, Monterey, Monterey County, California, 1968. Looking north along the main canning area. Retorts were located under the wooden framework on the right. *Documentation compiled after, photograph; Library of Congress, https://www.loc.gov/item/ca1292; photos from Survey HAER CA-11.*

It wasn't long before other migrants moved to the area after hearing about the salmon fishing the area had become known for. Japanese, Portuguese and Italian immigrants began flocking to the area and began fishing the waters off of the Monterey Peninsula. By the late 1800s, the Portuguese began shore-whaling (establishing lookouts high up on beaches to spot whales) and salmon fishing along the rocky shoreline and below the roadway near today's Cannery Row. However, it was the Italians who began arriving in large numbers around 1880. This pushed the Chinese out of their domination over the fishing industry of the Monterey Bay. After the third fire burned the Chinese settlement at China Point to the ground in 1906, the Chinese were removed as a major force in the fishing industry of the area. The arrival of the Italian population coincided with the arrival of the Southern Pacific Railroad and the construction of the Hotel Del Monte. The hotel, when opened in June 1880, quickly became known as the most lavish seaside resort in the world and ushered in the tourist trade for the once-sleepy town of Monterey, California.

Even though, at the turn of the 1900s, salmon was the primary fishing mainstay, the Monterey sardine was becoming a well-known commodity among fishermen, and its abundance in the bay made it hard to ignore. Larger than its East Coast kin, the Monterey sardine, once introduced to the market, became famous not only as a food source but also as a fertilizer and oil supply. Frank Booth built the first cannery in Monterey in 1895, near Fisherman's Wharf, mainly canning salmon. However, as many of the fishermen were now also harvesting the plentiful sardines of the bay, he began canning them as well. Booth was also the first canner to hire Sicilian fishermen, who used their lampara nets, which they introduced to California in 1905. The lampara net had been used in the Mediterranean with much success, and its ability to collect hundreds of thousands of sardines in a single troll was revolutionizing the fishing trade in Monterey.

By 1916, canneries were springing up all over Ocean View Avenue (the street's original name), with the first, Pacific Fish Company, having been established in February 1908. Even though these canneries were relatively small, they still produced the largest number of canned sardines in the world. Between 1908 and 1916, both fishing and canning techniques improved, which prepared Monterey's canneries for the huge spike in demand that was coming with the start of World War I. At the beginning of the Great War, the canning industry needed about a year to ramp up production, and by 1915, it was producing approximately 75,000 cases of sardines a year. By 1918, however, that number had reached a whopping 1.4 million. This war production was not only in foodstuffs but also in oil and fishmeal products. After the armistice of 1918, production decreased, but not by a substantial margin. With a major recession brought on by World War I, sardines, being relatively cheap, became a food staple. And as the slow economic recovery morphed into the exciting times of the Roaring Twenties, the stench of sardine packing and grinding into fishmeal continued and became known in Monterey as the "smell of prosperity."

Just before the Great Depression hit in 1929, Knut Hovden modernized the sardine fishing and canning industry in Monterey by introducing purse seiner fishing boats (boats that used large nets that could trap tons of fish in a single net), which greatly increased the number of fish brought in by

Historic American Engineering Record, creator, Knute Hovden, Stanford University, Wilbur Ellis Company, Pietro "Pete" Ferrante and William Lunde. Hovden Cannery, 886 Cannery Row, Monterey, Monterey County, California, 1968. Exterior of Hovden Cannery on Cannery Row. *Documentation compiled after, photograph; Library of Congress, https://www.loc.gov/item/ca1292; photos from Survey HAER CA-11.*

a single boat. He also replaced the bucket-and-cable transfer system that had been used by fishermen for generations to transfer their catch to the canneries. This old method was woefully inadequate to handle the number of fish being brought in nightly by the new nets. Hovden replaced the old transfer system by devising a floating wooden hopper that was anchored to the seabed and then connected to the canneries by steel pipes. On the other end of these hoppers were marine pumps that sucked the catch into the canneries for immediate processing or into holding tanks to be processed later. This new way of catching and transferring the boat's catch was not only revolutionary but also set the stage for the end of the fishing industry in Monterey.

Limping along through the Depression, Monterey's canneries were able to provide cheap food for a weary country. As the Depression began to end with the beginning of World War II, the canneries were once again called on to provide needed food and oil for the war effort. It was during this production boom of World War II that Monterey became known as the "sardine capital of the world." This moniker came about due to the canneries producing almost a quarter million tons of sardines per season during the peak wartime years. Using Hovden's new methods, Monterey's canners provided the world with enough foodstuffs, fish oil, fishmeal and other supplies to help with the war effort. Unfortunately, it also depleted the sardine population to the point that it would never recover. The Monterey sardines disappeared due to technology and overfishing.

By the mid-1950s, the sardine industry brought in less than one thousand tons of sardines a season. This was nowhere near the amount required to sustain the canning industry, and many canneries began to shut down, laying off workers by the hundreds. As the sardines' numbers declined, so did the canneries. And it wasn't long before Ocean View Avenue was nothing more than a ghost town, with virtually no canneries remaining. The area that was once the economic engine that drove Monterey began to collapse, its buildings disintegrating and falling into rubble. But Ocean View Avenue refused to die, and visionaries like Neil DeVaughn (1953), Kalisa Moore (1958) and Dick O'Kane (1963) opened their restaurants among the dying warehouses and kept the area on life support. But there is one man who gets the most credit for saving this piece of Americana from falling into the abyss of history and who, as a writer, made history and Cannery Row what it is today.

John Steinbeck was born in Salinas, California, only about thirty miles away from Ocean View Avenue and the Monterey canneries. After his marriage to Carol Henning in 1930, the couple moved to Pacific Grove, next to the fishing mecca. Steinbeck began to hang out and make friends with some of the characters who lived and worked among the canneries; one of these people, a marine biologist, ecologist and philosopher by the name of Ed Ricketts, would become a central figure in Steinbeck's masterful work of fiction *Cannery Row*. Living in a house owned by his father and spending his time around the canneries, Steinbeck was enthralled with the mix of people he encountered and the stories they told of life working as canners and fisherman. These stories were the catalysts for some of Steinbeck's most memorable literary characters. Steinbeck wrote his award-winning *Tortilla Flats* novel while living among these colorful personalities, but his mind kept coming back to what he called "cannery row" along the shore of Monterey Bay. As the 1940s dawned, Steinbeck's marriage was coming to an end, and after the divorce, he moved from Pacific Grove. Steinbeck may have left the canneries, but the canneries never left Steinbeck. In 1945, *Cannery Row* was published and became one of his most famous works. It is this book and its characters that saved what would come to be called Cannery Row.

Over the years, Cannery Row (Ocean View Avenue officially changed names in 1958 to honor Steinbeck) slowly became the tourist mecca we know today. Folks first came to see the canneries made famous by Steinbeck's novel, and then as upscale restaurants, souvenir shops, boutiques and curio markets grew, so did the tourist trade. When, in 1984, the Monterey Bay Aquarium opened in the old Hovden Cannery building, Monterey also became a worldwide attraction. In another nod to Steinbeck and his friend Ed Ricketts ("Doc" in the book), the aquarium embraced Ricketts's methods of marine biology that were set down in *Cannery Row* and used by Ricketts in his Pacific Laboratories, which was located next to what is now the aquarium. One thing that hasn't changed and never can is the history of hard, backbreaking work of the fishers and canners, the dangerous conditions they had to work under and the sacrifices they made to help feed the world. This may be one of the reasons that Cannery Row is said to be so haunted.

As we have seen, Cannery Row grew out of backbreaking, dangerous work. The men who worked the boats and canneries died in accidents, some during the Depression and other hard economic times. More died by suicide after they were laid off and the canneries were shut down when the fish disappeared. This type of suffering can and will bring about spirits who remain long after their bodies have decayed and turned to dust. One of these lost souls did not die from work, suicide or in a factory accident; rather, they had an unexplained death by train.

"Doc" Ricketts's lab is still next to the aquarium that adopted his methods in marine biology.

Ed Ricketts, as mentioned, was a central figure in Steinbeck's *Cannery Row* and, being a scientist, had a lab on the water side of Ocean Avenue, almost next door to what is now the Monterey Bay Aquarium. This lab is still there today and is reportedly haunted by Ricketts—and possibly a few of his friends. In 1948, Ricketts died a few blocks from his lab when he went to get food for a gathering he was having. Coming back from his errand, Ricketts's car stalled out on the train tracks that used to run to and from the fish canneries. Instead of getting out of his car, he continued to try to move it until the train hit the automobile and killed Ed Ricketts almost immediately. It is still a mystery why Ricketts didn't just leave his car and get out of the way of the moving train, whistle and all barreling down on him.

In season 2, episode 7 of the podcast *Spirits & Cousins: With Tish and Courtney* (January 18, 2024), the hosts talk about how folks will hear the sounds of a whistle coming from a phantom train heading down the now-missing tracks. And while there are reports of feeling the presence of Ricketts next to the memorial that was erected for him on the spot where he was killed, it's said you can also sometimes catch the sounds of a spectral woman sobbing right where Ricketts met his end. No one is sure who this mournful woman is, only that her sadness can be felt. The podcast also mentions that many folks believe Ricketts haunts his old lab. There are unsubstantiated rumors that Ricketts, Steinbeck and their friends were heavily into mysticism and would hold séances at the lab. It is also rumored that these mystic meetings may be the reason spirits still haunt the location. Strange lights are seen above the rickety front stairs, and many claim they've seen a shadowy figure emerging from the building late at night. This figure is seen walking down the stairs to the street and then strolling down Cannery Row before simply vanishing. It seems that "Doc" Ricketts may still be researching ocean life and the paranormal at Cannery Row to this day.

Steinbeck Plaza is about halfway down the street on the water side, and here, you will find shops, restaurants, tourist fare and where one used to find the fantastic Magic Wand Shop at Zucchini's. You will also find a photo shop that has a couple of resident spirits. Doc Wenzel's Old Time Portraits is your typical picture venue where you dress up in costumes from the Victorian era, as a character from the Wild West or any of another dozen periods to have your picture taken to impress your friends and family. What isn't typical about this tourist shop is the fact that when you get home, you may just find a ghost in your pictures. While talking with the manager of the photo studio, I found out that she believes there are two active spirits in the shop. One of these entities is named Robert, and he has been with the manager since her youth. The other has been named Harold because, as the manager says, "he just feels like a Harold."

The manager said that neither of these spirits is anything but playful, moving things around but never being destructive. She told me that one morning, while opening, she found one of the display pictures about eight feet away from the wall it usually hung from, face down on a rug. The yellow ribbon that is normally tied to the picture was no longer on the frame; instead, it was on the floor in front of the entrance to the shop. Another time—and this has happened on more than one occasion—the large, heavy area rug in the studio was found folded up. Sometimes, it has been folded more than once. One morning, they found the rug folded up like "a burrito."

The hats customers use for dress-up are all hung up on one rack, and they all have their own special hook so they can be easily found when needed. One of these hats has been known to fly off its hooks and land in the middle of the area rug. What makes this even more unusual is the fact that this hat is placed behind several other hats, but those other hats never seem to move. It is not uncommon for this hat to be placed back on its hook and then immediately fly back to the center of the rug, as if tossed by unseen hands. Other items will simply disappear from the desk or customer podium while they are still in use, and even customers have commented on how an item can simply vanish only a few seconds after being used.

The manager also told me that strange things happen within the mall in the hallways and nearby shops. She said that a light switch, which operates the space outside these shops, will suddenly just switch off, leaving the entire area in shadow and darkness. She will go to flip the switch back, but before she can blink an eye, the lights will be out again. After the manager demands the lights be left on, the perpetrator leaves them alone. Other strange things happen and have been confirmed by others who work inside the mall area; folks have seen people walking down the walkways and then simply vanish as they are viewed, shadows have darted about from place to place and the potted plants have moved as if someone brushed up against them. There is no wind within the enclosed mall that could explain this, which makes it even more eerie when witnessed. Folks have even seen reflections of people in the glass of storefronts, but once they turn around to look, there is no one there.

Across the street from the main Steinbeck Plaza is another, smaller mall. This mall has a glass elevator on the outside that takes folks up to the second floor, where they will find a liquor store, a skate shop and a large candy store. A few of the proprietors of these shops told me that the elevator will operate

The Wing Chong building remains, ghost and all.

even when no one has pressed the call button, and it will move between floors as if there are people inside. Maintenance workers cannot find any malfunction or any logical reason for the lift to operate without a human pressing the buttons. Those I spoke with also said that sometimes, when they are closing up and after the elevator has been shut down for the night, it will still operate as if it is bringing folks to the upper level, and the soft sound of someone walking away can be heard although no one can be seen.

Across the street from Doc Ricketts's lab is the old Wing Chong (meaning "glorious successful") Company Grocery building. This store was the inspiration for the Lee Chong Grocery in Steinbeck's *Cannery Row*. According to the "Final Cannery Row Cultural Resources Survey Report Document," prepared for the City of Monterey in 2001, the market was founded by Won Yee in 1934, and the market became almost like a company store for those who worked at the canneries. Not only did the market offer foodstuffs, but it also sold items like work gloves, fishing gear and other day-to-day things a canner may have needed. By 1937, the family had expanded to include the Yock H. Yee restaurant and had become an integral part of the community. Today, the market is gone and the building houses various shops, but it is still there and looks the same as it always did. Even the sign for the market still hangs from the building. Won Yee himself, although long dead, is said to still be there, looking after his store.

According to Tish and Courtney in their podcast, it is not uncommon to see dark figures coming out of the building. It is as if Yee's customers are still loyal to the market, the main shopping venue for the workers in the nearby canneries. Won Yee used to sit in his market and tap his knuckles on the countertop, a habit that some believed was a nervous tic. It is well known that if you go into the store after nightfall, you can still hear Yee and his knuckles tapping away on the countertop. Folks will look around for the source of the tapping, but no one can be seen where the sound appears to be emanating from. It's thought that Yee, who was a very important member of the community, is still there looking after his market and his customers.

Today, Cannery Row has become a tourist mecca.

The rancid smell of fish guts and oil is long gone from Monterey's Cannery Row. The canneries have been transformed into upscale restaurants and tourist shops, and the cannery workers have been replaced by travelers from around the world. What hasn't changed and what still remains is the image of John Steinbeck's *Cannery Row*, many of the historic buildings and the spirit that made Cannery Row the "sardine capital of the world." It's not only the spirit of the town but the spirits that still "live" in the town.

Mission San Carlos Borroméo de Carmelo

The Carmel Mission's actual name is Mission San Carlos Borroméo de Carmelo, but it has become "Americanized" with the name Carmel Mission for so many years now that no one remembers its true name. The second mission to be set up by the colonizing Spaniards, the Carmel Mission would become the headquarters for all of the missions in Alta (upper) California. "History is written by the victors" is an apt statement for most of the missions in California, as the history of such is only half true and omits many of the horrors that the California tribes had to deal with in their "conversion" to Christianity.

Founded shortly after Serra and Captain Portola landed in Monterey on June 3, 1770, the mission, along with the presidio, began the conversion of the local people. The Spanish troops at the presidio mistreated the local population, and the people who associated the mission with the fort began to seriously distrust the padres, as well as Father Serra. Much of this may have been due to the priests turning a blind eye to what their Spanish brethren were doing. Even after Father Serra moved the mission to its new, present location, the people were still wary of the missionaries. As I mentioned in my book *Ghosts and Legends of Alcatraz*, the Northern Californian people believed Alcatraz was a place of evil, with an evil creature inhabiting the land, and they would mostly avoid the island unless they were dropping off exiled tribesmen. As scared as they were of the island, the people hid there to get away from the forced conversion the Spaniards pressed on them. I will leave it up to my readers to decide what they believe of Father Serra and the mission system.

The Basilica today.

Even though many of the tribes shied away from the missionaries, some of their people were brought into the fold on their own accord—and others somewhat forcibly. The treatment of Natives at the missions was varied, with some of them treating the tribesmen as slaves. This caused revolts at many missions, some deadly. Others treated the Native people sternly yet fairly. The Carmel Mission was somewhere in between. The Carmel Mission flourished, as the new location provided rich agricultural opportunities and a clean, constant water source and was farther from the soldiers stationed at the presidio. Even though the five to seven Spanish soldiers who were stationed at the mission still had distain for the Native people, they were under the stronger control of the two to three padres who ran the mission. After Father Serra passed away in 1884, the Carmel Mission came under the control of Padre Fermín de Lasuén.

It was Lasuén who built the mission church (basilica) we see today, but he also had a past that included ignoring the raping of the Kumeyaay tribe's women and the stealing of their food, which led to the tribe attacking the San Diego Mission. Father Serra was there at the time and stated that he "prayed to God to give victory to our Holy Catholic faith without the loss of a single soul." Lasuén, ever the diplomat, was always open with those in the Spanish military and never minced words when trying to get the needs of the mission met by those in the government. However, his letters to the military commanders made him no friends, as he often suggested how they should deploy their troops and the formations that should be used during a march. The military began to push back, which was both a blessing and detriment to the mission. It was a detriment in that the presidio was more likely to ignore a call for help, and it was a blessing in that they stayed out of the way of the running of the mission.

Shortly after the new basilica was dedicated in 1797, a decline in the number of neophytes occurred. This was partly the result of the California mission headquarters being transferred to Santa Barbara after Lasuén's death in 1803. This decline continued, and by 1834, when the Mexican government secularized the mission, the number of neophytes was down to its lowest number since the mission was founded. Then in 1846, Governor Pio Pico offered the basilica up for sale, but by that time, the church had deteriorated so far that it was nothing more than a ruin. In 1852, the roof finally collapsed; the tiles and other usable material were taken and used in other structures, and it seemed as if the Mission San Carlos Borroméo de Carmelo would be lost to history.

When the United States gained control of California after the Mexican-American War ended in 1848, the push for statehood was intense. After Congress, the president and, more importantly, the people of the United States granted California statehood in 1850, it took only a short while and pressure from the Catholic Church for the government to give control of the mission system back to the church. Although the basilica was all but destroyed, a new roof was installed in 1884 to help keep it from further erosion, and it was rededicated as a church. After that, albeit slowly, reconstruction began. Full restoration didn't begin until the 1920s, but in the haste to get the job done, historical considerations took a backseat.

Historic American Buildings Survey, creator, and Serra. Mission San Carlos Borroméo, Rio Road and Lausen Drive, Carmel-by-the-Sea, Monterey County, California, 1933. *Documentation compiled after, photograph; Library of Congress, https://www.loc.gov/item/ca0361.*

However, since the early to mid-1930s, as more funds rolled in, more careful research has been done, and reconstruction from a historical point of view was followed. Native building materials have been used and details of the original structure have been incorporated, so what we see today is as close to the true original basilica as possible.

Today, the façade and portions of the stone walls of the church are original; however, the structure and all the other buildings at the mission complex are reconstructions. The most ornate façade has a star-shaped window of Moorish design, and the church is furnished with the original stone font where the tribesmen were baptized. The paintings and statues in the basilica are original and were returned to the building as part of the reconstruction program. Before the altar are situated the graves of Fathers Crespi and Lasuén. Father Serra's grave is located in a room by itself; he was interred in an ornate crypt that can be viewed by tourists who visit the Carmel Mission.

The California Mission System was obviously not perfect. Some of the problems were related to the prejudices of the time, as the Spanish thought that only European people were "civilized." The Spanish soldiers thought they could mistreat the tribesmen and have their way with the tribeswomen. Many neophytes were treated as slaves, forced to toil long hours with few breaks, and then "converted" away from their own beliefs. Many of the padres did not like the treatment the neophytes received but remained obedient to their superiors' orders. With the way many of these people were treated and the many deaths that occurred with no thought to the death rights of the tribe's beliefs, it should come as no surprise that the Carmel Mission has a few restless spirits that have not been able to move into the afterlife.

Since Padre Serra was the one to establish the mission system and lived at the Carmel Mission for so long, and since he was buried in front of the sanctuary altar, it is not surprising that many folks believe he is still at the mission. In his book *Haunted Monterey County* (The History Press, 2019), Patrick Whitehurst says that Junípero Serra has been seen numerous times, walking the grounds of the mission. And he has been known to return every year on the Feast of San Carlos to say mass. The mission is named in honor of Carlos Borroméo. Whitehurst goes on to say that Serra was buried at the foot of the sanctuary altar, and since that time, sightings of strange, fog-like beings have been reported in and around the mission. These reports come more frequently during the feast. Even after the old church where Serra was buried collapsed, these eerie figures were seen and have continued to appear since it was rebuilt with stones quarried from the local mountains, along with usable pieces of the original buildings. The reused bricks and stone may also be the catalysts for another strange tale of Padre Serra's spirit.

On the website *Seeks Ghosts*, there is a tale about the "Tripping Stones" of the Carmel Mission. According to legend, in the 1860s, a person at the mission, most likely while looking for something to steal, suddenly tripped as he approached what was left of the altar. Even though the floor was even and uncluttered, he fell hard to his knees, facing the cross, as if he was about to pray. After this and after he told others what had happened, folks began whispering that it had not been an accident that this happened to him. In the following years, people began to notice this type of thing happening to others who visited the mission. After restoration, the sanctuary floor remained smooth and even, yet those who enter with disrespect have found themselves "tripping" on something unseen, falling to their knees right on the spot where Padre Serra is interred. Many people now believe that Father Serra himself is keeping an eye on the mission and trying to teach proper respect for the faith to those who lack reverence. Even today, folks who walk into the sanctuary who show a lack of respect will find themselves tripping and falling into a praying position when near the grave of Junípero Serra. If these tales are true, Padre Serra is still manning the mission and making sure neophytes honor his commands.

The mission cemetery is one of those places where truth and legend combine to tell a tale of heartache and ghosts. There are two distinct areas, with the padres and church elite buried along the basilica wall in a pristine garden setting and the neophytes buried across the way in a somewhat tended dirt area. It is in this area where Native people were buried, and even though they may not have converted to Catholicism, they were buried in that faith,

Father Serra's crypt.

not their own. This can bring about restless spirits who walk the Earth. It is also said that bodies were buried on top of bodies here, which can produce the same result. Maybe this is why the cemetery of the mission is said to be the most haunted area of the complex. Here, folks have seen apparitions of tribe members, many who seem to be confused by their surroundings. Shadow figures are common, and strange sounds have been heard during the nighttime hours here. A young boy has been seen wandering around the cemetery, but he has also been seen in other areas of the mission grounds. This is also common with other phantoms of the mission, as many have even been seen outside the mission walls.

Other strange phenomena that are experienced at the mission include folks who feel disembodied hands brushing up against them as if trying to touch the living and at other times these hands lightly grasp unsuspecting guests with what they say feel like an ice cube freezing their skin. There is even a phantom rider and horse that is seen. According to Whitehurst, this specter rides a glowing white stallion and speeds through the grounds, always heading south to the Santa Lucia Mountains. Many believe this rider could be none other than Joaquin Murrieta, who became known as

Creepy Jesus.

the Robin Hood of El Dorado and was the inspiration for the fictional Mexican hero Zorro. There are so many stories surrounding Murrieta that many believe most of the myths serve to boost the reputation of an outlaw. No one is truly sure who the ghostly rider is, and as he rides so fast, identifying him is impossible; we may never know the answer. It is also said that the rider is actually headless, but these tales are few and far between, and as many of the missions in the California Mission System lay claim to headless priests or Spanish soldiers, it could be a simple mix-up of tales that decapitates this rider.

The Mission San Carlos Borroméo de Carmelo is in one of the most beautiful locations of any of the missions in the system. It, like most of the California missions, has had its ups and downs, as well as deaths associated with mission life—those of the tribes more than most. Its history is that of not only faith and conversion but also hard labor and death; this is the same with all of the missions and most likely the reason they all have ghosts reported on their grounds.

Hauntable Mention

Mount Shasta's McCloud River B+B

(As reported in the *Mt. Shasta News*, November 11, 2008, by Gene Eagle)

When new owners purchased the McCloud Century House and began restoring the historic hotel (the hotel was also McCloud's first hospital), strange things began to happen. They began to suspect that the old place was haunted when they heard the sound of footsteps in the hallway and on the stairs when no one was there and when they saw a dark figure standing in the hallway that simply disappeared as they watched. Even the guests began reporting eerie things happening in the old inn. The owners finally called in a local paranormal team to try to get to the bottom of what was going on in their bed-and-breakfast. During their investigation, the team witnessed shadow figures throughout the hotel, saw a dark figure walking up the stairway and heard disembodied footsteps. One investigator even heard a spirit say out loud, "I'm alright."

The team never did find out if the activity was caused by a single or multiple entities, but considering the bed-and-breakfast was a former hospital, it isn't hard to believe that there could be quite a few spirits lingering in the historic hotel. Mt. Shasta has a history of strange and eerie things going on, and the McCloud B&B fits right into that category, which is great for paratravelers and adventure seekers alike. As a note, the McCloud Mercantile Hotel is another inn that has a reputation for paranormal activity, so if there is no room at the inn, the hotel is a great alternative.

ALTURAS' NILES HOTEL

(AS REPORTED IN THE *LOS ANGELES TIMES*, MAY 26, 2023, BY HAILEY BRANSON-POTTS)

The small northern town of Alturas, California, may have one of the most haunted hotels in the state. The Niles Hotel, situated in the remote northeastern corner of California, is said to be haunted by the spirit of a slain soiled dove. Although, according to one of the bartenders, the ghost of this sex worker does not like men, she is known to crawl into bed with them while they are sleeping. Maybe she is still trying to earn her keep at the hotel and thinks she must be with the men, which could be a reason why she doesn't like them much. This spirit is also fond of scratching on the walls and stomping the floors, keeping folks, mostly men, awake at night. The owners welcome paranormal investigators, and they themselves have had a few experiences. He said that once, his wife was working on the third floor when, right in front of her face, a woman appeared. She was there for only a second before she vanished, but she looked as solid as any person would.

The Haunted Eureka Inn.

The hotel bar seems to have its share of activity as well. The bartender said that one evening, a male guest came down and said that he had been woken by something tugging on his pillow. He said that when he rolled over to get up, something pushed him down and held him in place. When the guest held out his arm to brush his face, the hairs on his arm stood straight up. Many folks are creeped out by the pictures on the walls of the bar; most are original Victorian paintings, and it is not unusual for people to complain that these paintings are staring at them and follow them when they move. One longtime patron said that since the construction work, things have ramped up, and now things will turn up missing, only to be found in another location; doors will open on their own; rooms will suddenly become ice cold; and strange whistling music will be heard coming from everywhere and nowhere. This is another place that should be added to a paratraveler's California bucket list.

EUREKA INN AND OLD TOWN COFFEE + CHOCOLATES

I had been drawn to the Eureka Inn with the promise of ghost stories but was unfortunately misled by the person who made the promise; however, others were not as reluctant to tell their tales. The Elizabethan Tudor Revival Eureka Inn was built in 1922 and is now listed in the National Register of Historic Places. Over the years, it has hosted many famous celebrities, such as Shirley Temple and Steven Spielberg, along with royalty and dignitaries, like Winston Churchill and Ronald Reagan. The hotel has had ups and downs and had been closed for years, but it has now reopened to serve guests, both alive and dead.

Staying at the Eureka Inn was like visiting a quaint English country inn, replete with ghosts, one of which is known to have a completely white face and wear a top hat. This spirit can usually be found near the hotel bar and will watch patrons as they socialize, have their drinks and enjoy each other's company. If one of the living happens to spot this dapper gentleman phantom, he will glance over, give a smile and vanish from sight. There is a display on the stairway landing outside the hotel's restaurant that holds a top hat, and many wonder if this hat is the reason for the well-dressed ghost.

Another ghost at the hotel likes to hang out in the ornate, expansive lobby. Most who have encountered this spirit say that he is not exactly the nicest ghost one could meet. While not overly aggressive, this specter is known to

This top hat may be that of one of the spirits of the Eureka Inn.

slap folks' backs; mildly shove people if they happen to be in his way, which is impossible for folks to figure out; and show himself in the fireplace on cold winter nights while people sit in the comfortable chairs and couches to enjoy one another's companionship. It would seem that there is also a spirit who resides on the third floor, but evidence is hard to find with only cursory details to go by.

In historic downtown, or Old Town Eureka, there is the Old Town Coffee & Chocolate shop. We went in here to grab a bit of breakfast since we had heard they had great donuts and pastries. Not only did we find this to be true, but we also managed to get a couple of good ghost stories. One of the clerks told us that there are always strange things afoot in the stockroom and behind the counter of this bakery. The staff are always hearing the sounds of things being moved around in the back room, where the customer and crew bathroom is located, but when they go back to take a look, they can find nothing amiss. The clerk said that the noise is sometimes loud enough that it sounds as if things are being knocked over. Footsteps are also heard in this same area, even when all living souls are accounted for out front.

Apple fritters.

The same cannot be said for the area behind the counter. The clerk said that there are times when they are preparing drinks that they turn to grab some cream, caramel or other drink requirements, and when they turn back around, the drink itself has been moved from where it had been only seconds earlier. The same thing will happen when they are setting donuts or pastries on the prep table and reach up for the powdered sugar, cinnamon or other needed topping; they will find it somewhere it should not be, and then after moving it back to its proper place, they will find it moved again the next time they reach for it. Even if you are not looking for the paranormal in this coffee shop, keep in mind that they have one of the best—if not the best—apple fritters I have ever eaten.

Just around the corner from the coffee shop is the Greene Lily Café. This used to be the Oberon Grill, made famous by a bar fight between author Jack London and future owner of the Pacific Lumber Company Stanwood Murphy. It's known to be haunted by a young woman who is believed to have died in Eureka's June 6, 1932 earthquake; this lady, it would seem, is not shy in the afterlife. Eureka is not only a beautiful coastal city, but it is also one that has a good number of spirits enjoying the scenery, seafood and ambiance.

FERNDALE

Ferndale, just below the city of Eureka, is known for its Victorian houses and architecture, and for some, it's known for its ghosts. While visiting, I could not find many stories, but I did hear about the Ferndale Repertoire Theater, which I thought very interesting. It would seem that a woman, possibly a ninety-eight-year-old who passed away in 1972, haunts the theater—but mostly as a cat. This feline female is also known to haunt the theater's bathrooms but as her true self.

The Gingerbread B&B is another place that seems to have a spirit or two (I had been told by townsfolk that it did). I went to the door and asked the owner, who was reluctant to speak with me until I mentioned why I asked. She invited me in but would not admit to the place being haunted. But I figured it must be after she mentioned she didn't want the ghosts to be offended by being in a book. Haunted or not, the Gingerbread House is beautiful, well-kept and within walking distance of downtown. It would be a wonderful location from which to explore the town.

One other location in town is the historic Ivanhoe Hotel. This hotel has been closed for quite a while, but it is in the process of being restored. I was lucky enough to go inside when I was there, and I was told by the work crew that some very strange things have been going on since they began working. They have seen shadow figures moving about, their tools have been moved to odd locations within the building, disembodied footsteps have been heard all over the building, and even a strange voice and unknown conversations have been heard. Once featured on *Diners, Drive-ins and Dives* (Guy Fieri grew up in Ferndale), this hotel and eatery, once opened, should be added to any paratraveler's list to check out.

LEGEND OF BIGFOOT STORE

This gift shop, literally in the middle of nowhere in Garberville, California, pops up right in front of your car as you drive along Highway 101, heading to or from Eureka. The bright colors of the store, along with the giant Sasquatch statue out front, make it impossible to miss. This gift shop capitalizes on the many reports from over one hundred years of Bigfoot being seen in the forests that surround the store. The Legend of Bigfoot has been owned by the Carlson family for well over forty years and has, in

Above: The Legend of Bigfoot Store.

Opposite: The Colfax Hotel.

that time, created one of the most unique gift stores found anywhere. Here, travelers can find fun and amusing signs, gifts made from local redwood trees, garden gnomes and other cryptid statues and, of course, more Bigfoot paraphernalia than you can imagine. There is even a treehouse for those who stop in for the incredible opportunity to snap pictures of the surrounding redwoods.

For those Bigfoot hunters among the paratraveler family, there are many campsites around the area to use as a staging site for your adventures, and a great place to start is the Legend of Bigfoot store itself. With books on the subject as well as maps, what Bigfoot hunter could ask for more? And for those simply passing by, this is a must-stop location for a bit of fun on your long drive to haunted adventures.

COLFAX HOTEL

While driving through the small town of Colfax, California, I decided to stop into the library to ask about any hauntings on Main Street. The staff was very friendly and open, yet they really couldn't tell me much other than there were shops that they knew to be haunted. But the shop owners would not want their stories told. I asked about the large white

building across the railroad tracks from the main square and found out that was the old Colfax Hotel that has been closed for years, even though many owners have tried to revive the old building. They told me it has gone through numerous owners since its closure, and each one has started renovations but stopped shortly after work began. The library staff went on to say that work crews always complained about their tools turning up missing, things falling over even though they were well secured and power tools mysteriously shutting down and not working again until they were out of the hotel. The workers would begin to hear strange voices, footsteps, knocks, bangs and other eerie noises, and some of them refused to go back into the building except to gather their tools and personal items before quitting the job. The current owners are trying to reopen the hotel now but are starting to run into the same problems. Let's hope that they can soon get this hotel open so all of my intrepid paratravelers have a new location, Colfax, to check out in the future.

LOCKE

The tiny town of Locke, California, is known as the only town in the country that was built by the Chinese for the Chinese. However, today, this claim has become mired in controversy, with some folks claiming the town's heritage is anything but Chinese. Others steadfastly believe the legends that have sprung up from those Chinese Americans who live in the town and can trace their heritage back to the town's founding in 1915. I will not wade into the fray, as it is not necessary to tell the story of the lost souls who remain in this unique and charming community. Some of the tales say that the Tong (the Chinese mafia) had a hand in creating the town and brought drugs, prostitution and violence to the community. While this may be true, not one person I spoke to in town ever mentioned the Tong in our conversations. If organized crime was a figure in Locke, the Di Loy Museum would be the place to find them.

A gambling hall turned museum, the Di Loy has quite the shady past. As such, it now has a ghostly reputation as a place where folks will see shadows darting just at the edge of their vision, where strange sounds emanate from empty rooms and people, mostly women, have been known to be violently shoved and men scratched. Rumor has it that someone was killed in the casino; the angry spirit may be the murderer, the victim or

Above: The Dai Loy Museum.

Left: Al the Wops Bar.

both. The Star Theater is another place in Locke that is said to have a few spirits, one of which is said to be that of a kind and light-filled Chinese singer. The others, however, are not. One, who supposedly resides in the attic storage area, gives off what some say is an odd and creepy feeling that imparts fear, and the other, which dwells in the basement, causes terror in those who enter his domain.

By far my favorite haunted spot is Al the Wops Bar. The bartender told me that Al opened the bar in 1934 and passed away in the bar in 1961. Since that day, patrons have been seeing Al still tending to the bar. The bartender told me that he has seen Al only once, walking across the floor as he was talking to "the village idiot and a traveling guy," but because the spirit was wearing the suit Al was buried in and walked in the same way as the deceased man, there was no mistaking him for anyone else. The bartender also told me that a longtime patron and town elder passed away after having an exorcism performed to get rid of a ghost in his house. Folks in town believe that the spirit, unfazed by the ritual, killed the man out of spite. Politics and town drama aside, the residents of Locke firmly believe the town is haunted, and even those who argue about the town's founding agree on this point.

FELTON COVERED BRIDGE

As my sister Maureen once lived in the small town of Felton, only a stone's throw from the haunted Brookdale Lodge, I had seen this covered bridge many times. While driving through on one of my many research trips, I decided to talk to one of the folks who lived next to the bridge. The local, Skeeter, told me that as the bridge used to be the only way in or out of Felton, bandits used to waylay folks on either end, rob them and, many times, kill them if they tried to resist. This, according to Skeeter, has caused a lot of activity here. He said that his neighbor once had what felt like sleep paralysis, but as he felt tentacles and could move slightly, he immediately knew it was something else. He said he began to do short little sit-ups, which began to release the tentacles. As the sit-ups got stronger and stronger, the tentacles went away. They both believe that it was a spirit from the bridge that held him in thrall. Skeeter also said that because Felton and the bridge are located deep in the forest, there are a lot of strange creatures that are seen there. He said reports of dogmen are very common. Bigfoot is a frequent guest at the bridge, as are skinwalkers. The strangest cryptid Skeeter mentioned

Felton's covered bridge.

This page: The Brookdale's haunted restaurant.

was that of a deer with a human face that is seen in the area so often that folks consider it normal. The Felton Covered Bridge is considered the tallest covered bridge in the country, and it is still open, but only for pedestrian traffic. And with its surrounding park and beautiful forest, it should not be missed if you are heading up to the famous and wonderfully haunted Brookdale Lodge.

The Tuttle Mansion

This elegant 1899 Queen Anne mansion was built by Morris Tuttle for his family. With six bedrooms, a family room, library, parlor, foyer, kitchens and more, the Tuttle Mansion became the talk of Watsonville. The Tuttles and those who followed lived a comfortable life, but the house itself seemed to hide a streak of bad luck. Over the years, the house has been an apartment and office building and home to several other businesses. The bizarre misfortunes began when one of the Tuttles' sons passed away at a young age. A murder took place in the carriage house, a murder-suicide occurred in one of the bedrooms, a boy fell to his death in the home's well and various other incidents have occurred here. This has caused the home, as some say, to become a portal to the afterlife and the most haunted house in Santa Cruz County.

The current owners, twin sisters Kathy and Jennifer Oliver, are not squeamish about talking about the ghosts and have said that Morris Tuttle himself is often seen looking out of the large second-story window, while his wife, Mary, has been spotted at the back of the house. A small boy spirit is thought to be that of their deceased son. Local investigators and friends of the Oliver sisters Paul Tashiro and Cherie Pruitt have been investigating the mansion for a while now, and some of the things they have found are chilling and heartbreaking. Paul and Cherie believe that the spirit of a young woman who lived in the 1930s or '40s is stuck at the home, waiting with a broken heart for a love she can never have. They believe this sad young lady is Alice Tuttle, Morris Tuttle's niece. Alice was tragically killed during a hunting accident when a rifle discharged and shot her in the face. According to Paul and Cherie, when Alice was a young girl, her father, Owen Tuttle, shot and killed her mother and then went to a bedroom upstairs and shot himself.

With the tragedy that has occurred in the Tuttle Mansion, one can see why it gained the title of the most haunted house in Santa Cruz County.

As Paul and Cherie stated, "This woman and many other spirits roam the hallways and rooms of the Tuttle Mansion, some waiting for their story to be heard, while others walk the halls endlessly haunting the storied mansion." Let us all hope that someday, the lost souls of this beautiful Queen Anne home find peace.

MOUNT MADONNA INN

Not many folks have heard of the Mount Madonna Inn, situated between Watsonville and Gilroy along Hecker Pass Road, and this is not surprising because the inn has been closed for more than two decades. However, Mount Madonna, Hecker Road and the inn have a dark and haunted past. Over the years, this stretch of beautiful road has seen horrendous car accidents, gruesome murders and body dumps, suicides and the tragic 1875 death of Sarah Miller, the eight-year-old daughter of the wealthy rancher and one-time largest landowner in the country, Henry Miller. Sarah fell off of her horse and passed away, but witnesses say that the spirit of Sarah has never left. Sarah has been spotted riding her horse all over the mountain and near the inn. Many folks have seen what they call (of course) the Lady in White,

The Mount Madonna Inn.

and many believe that this, too, is Sarah. However, a senior park ranger believes that the Lady in White is not Sarah Miller but the spirit of a brutally murdered pregnant teenager, Sara Chavaria. Sara was viciously killed by her boyfriend in 1969 at the Mount Madonna Park entrance.

Over the years and even before the inn shuttered its doors, those driving by and those dining at the inn have reported seeing strange figures walking aimlessly before simply vanishing from sight. They've also heard eerie voices that sound as if they are coming from right beside them and the sound of horse's hooves, as if Sarah Miller is riding past in her afterlife. Perhaps the most alarming are the calls for help that come from all around and nowhere at the same time. The inn, in its state of decay, gives off an eerie vibe. It gives one the feeling that they are being watched from windows that no longer exist. And in the twilight of evening, it makes folks' skin crawl, and goosebumps form. Perfect for any paratraveler.

Toro Place Café

I found this place by accident, and after eating here, I have put it on my must-return list. While heading home from Monterey, we were looking for a place to stop for breakfast, and since we were driving down the highly

The Toro Place Café.

unpopulated State Route 68 (Monterey Salinas Highway) we were not very optimistic. However, right in front of us there appeared a parking lot packed with cars—always a good sign. And then we spotted the Toro Place Café. Not sure what to expect, we were surprised to find a wide selection of both Mexican and American breakfast items, and we were very pleased with how good the food tasted. It was also a nice surprise to find out the café was haunted. I mean, every paratraveler needs to eat, right? There seems to be only one spirit at this café, but our server said they have named the ghost The Cowboy because he wears a cowboy hat and clothes reminiscent of a ranch hand (there are many farms and ranches in the area). She told us that The Cowboy is not shy about letting folks know he is there and will show himself often, always giving diners a smile, a nod and a tip of the hat before wandering off or disappearing. After our fantastic meal, it is clear why The Cowboy stays at the café. Keep an eye out for the Toro Place Café if you are driving from Monterey to the 101 Freeway. Stop in—you won't regret it.

BIBLIOGRAPHY

PODCASTS

Whitcraft, Courtney, and Tish Whitcraft, hosts. *Spirits & Cousins*, podcast. Season 1, episode 6, "The Fort Ord Investigation." June 27, 2023. https://podcasts.apple.com/us/podcast/episode-6-the-fort-ord-investigation/id1671385475?i=1000618435194.

———. *Spirits & Cousins*, podcast. Season 2, episode 7, "Haunted Cannery Row." June 18, 2024. https://www.buzzsprout.com/2104771/episodes/15271574-haunted-cannery-row?t=0.

———. *Spirits & Cousins*, podcast. Season 2, episode 7, "Haunted Monterey." June 4, 2024. https://www.buzzsprout.com/2104771/episodes/15195329-haunted-monterey?t=0.

CANNERY ROW

"The Canneries." Cannery Row. https://canneryrow.com/our-story/the-canneries.

McMahon, Heather N. "Wing Chong Building." SAH Archipedia. Society of Architectural Historians. https://sah-archipedia.org/buildings/CA-01-053-0015-07.

CARMEL MISSION

"Carmel Mission." National Park Service. https://www.nps.gov/places/carmel-mission.htm.

"Carmel Mission, California." Survey of Historic Sites and Buildings. National Park Service. https://www.nps.gov/parkhistory/online_books/explorers/sitec5.htm.

Lamkin, Virginia. "Carmel Mission: The Mysterious Tripping Stone." *Seeks Ghosts*. May 20, 2015. https://seeksghosts.blogspot.com/2015/05/carmel-mission-mysterious-tripping-stone.html.

CASTLE AIR MUSEUM

"Brigadier General Frederick W. Castle." Air Force. https://www.af.mil/About-Us/Biographies/Display/Article/108537/brigadier-general-frederick-w-castle.

"Castle Air Force Base (Air Corps Basic Flying School-Merced, Merced Army Air Field, Castle Field)." Historic California Posts, Camps, Stations and Airfields. https://www.militarymuseum.org/CastleAFB.html.

"History of Castle AFB." Air Force Civil Engineer Center. https://www.afcec.af.mil/Home/BRAC/Castle/History.

DELTA KING

"The Steamboats *Delta King* and *Delta Queen* (Part 1: History)." *The Ocean Liner Blogger*. October 20, 2010. https://oceanlinerblog.blogspot.com/2010/10/steamboats-delta-king-and-delta-queen.html?m=1.

EUREKA INN

Maxwell, Rose. "The Eureka Inn, Eureka, CA." The Haunted Hovel. http://www.hauntedhovel.com/the-eureka-inn-eureka-ca.html.

FORT ORD

Fort Ord historian. "History of Fort Ord, 1917–1972." California Military Department Historical Program. February 1974. https://www.militarymuseum.org/History%20of%20Fort%20Ord%201917-1972.pdf.

Krenzelok, Greg. Honoring Ord's History. https://freepages.rootsweb.com/~gregkrenzelok/genealogy/veterinary%20corp%20in%20ww1/honoringftordhistorydec32009.html.

JACKSON

"The History of the Kennedy Mine." Historic Kennedy Gold Mine. https://kennedygoldmine.com/history/.

"Jackson Mining History." City of Jackson, California. https://www.ci.jackson.ca.us/visit_jackson/mining_history.php.

Rasmussen, Cecilia. "1922 Gold Mine Disaster Was State's Deadliest." *Los Angeles Times*, January 15, 2006. https://www.latimes.com/archives/la-xpm-2006-jan-15-me-then15-story.html.

LOCKE

Rebmann, Dana. "A Ghost Town Near Sacramento Contains Little Known California History." 7x7. November 13, 2012. https://www.7x7.com/a-ghost-town-near-sacramento-contains-little-known-california-history-1781796785.html.

MOUNT MADONNA

"Legends of Mt. Madonna." "Legends" Santa Cruz Ghost Hunters. https://www.santacruzghosthunters.com/the-mount-madonna-inn.html.

NEVADA CITY, GRASS VALLEY

"The Ancestral Homelands of the Nisenan." Nisenan. https://www.nisenan.org.

"The Early History of Nevada City." Nevada City History. https://nevadacityhistory.com/history/early-history.php.

"Grass Valley History." Grass Valley Downtown Association. https://downtowngrassvalley.com/grass-valley-history.

NCS Import. "'Ghost Man' Appears on 'My Ghost Story' (video)." *The Union*, August 4, 2010. https://www.theunion.com/news/local-news/ghost-man-appears-on-my-ghost-story-video/article_ca7125c7-6208-5115-af7c-0c8e3a5d69cf.html.

"Nevada City History." Nevada City Chamber of Commerce. https://www.nevadacitychamber.com/history/california-history.

Nevada City Rancheria. https://nevadacityrancheria.org.

"Our Community History." Greater Grass Valley Chamber of Commerce. https://www.grassvalleychamber.com/community/history.

Phaneuf, Whitney. "8 Haunted Spots in California's Gold Country: Head Up the 'Golden Chain,' Highway 49, in Search of Haunted History." AAA. September 5, 2023. https://mwg.aaa.com/via/places-visit/haunted-california-gold-country.

OLD SACRAMENTO

"Delta King." Clio. https://theclio.com/entry/86348.

"Eagle Theater." California State Parks. https://www.parks.ca.gov/?page_id=27174.

Mortensen, Ricky, host. *Ricky's Historical Tidbits*, podcast. Episode 5, "May Woolsey—The Trunk Under the Stairs." https://www.rickyshistoricaltidbits.com/podcast/may-woolsey-the-trunk-under-the-stairs.

"Sacramento, California, United States. *Encyclopædia Britannica*. https://www.britannica.com/place/Sacramento-California.

PRESTON CASTLE, IONE

"Historic Haunt: Spirits Creep Around Preston Castle." *San Joaquin*, September 2020. https://sanjoaquinmagazine.com/2020/09/historic-haunt.

"Historic Ione." City of Ione, California. https://www.ione-ca.com/about-ione/page/historic-ione.

Historic Preston Restoration Foundation. https://historicprestonfoundation.org/default.aspx.

Womack, Graham. "Once-Abandoned Castle Looms Over a Small California Town. Its Story Is Spooky and Redeeming." *The Sacramento Bee*, September 19, 2024. https://www.sacbee.com/news/local/history/article291051915.html.

SANTA CRUZ BOARDWALK

Conard, Kristin. "One of the World's Best Seaside Parks Is in This Vibrant California City." Islands. June 24, 2024. https://www.islands.com/1604725/worlds-best-seaside-park-vibrant-california-city-santa-cruz-boardwalk.

Hukill, Traci. "The Santa Cruz Beach Boardwalk: A Look Back in Time." Santa Cruz County. https://www.santacruz.org/blog/beach-boardwalk-a-look-back-in-time.

Walking Tour of the Historic Santa Cruz Beach Boardwalk. Santa Cruz Beach Boardwalk. https://beachboardwalk.com/wp-content/uploads/2024/02/Boardwalk-Walking-Tour-02272024_web.pdf.

USS *HORNET*

USS *Hornet* CV/CVA/CVS-12 Ghost Stories. https://www.its.caltech.edu/~drmiles/ghost_stories.html.

"USS *Hornet* (CV 12)." U.S. Carriers. December 9, 2010. http://www.uscarriers.net/cv12history.htm.

WINCHESTER HOUSE

Davis, Mary. "Sarah Winchester & the 2,000 Doors." *Heroes, Heroines & History*. January 23, 2020. https://www.hhhistory.com/2020/01/sarah-winchester-2000-doors.html?m=1.

Dowd, Katie. "Everything You Think You Know About the Winchester Mystery House Probably Isn't True." SFGATE. October 31, 2021. https://www.sfgate.com/sfhistory/article/the-myth-of-the-winchester-mystery-house-16571653.php.

"A Haunted History." Winchester Mystery House. September 30, 2019. https://winchestermysteryhouse.com/a-haunted-history.

"Sarah Winchester Biography." Biography.com. August 4, 2020. https://www.biography.com/personality/sarah-winchester.

About the Author

Brian Clune is a cofounder and the historian for Planet Paranormal Investigations and has traveled the entire state of California researching its haunted hot spots and historical locations in an effort to bring knowledge of the paranormal and the wonderful history of the state to those interested in learning.

His interest in history has led him to volunteer aboard the USS *Iowa*, and he gives lectures at colleges, universities and events around the state. Brian has been involved with numerous TV shows, including *Ghost Adventures*, *My Ghost Story*, *Dead Files* and *Ghost Hunters*, and was the subject in a companion documentary for the movie *Paranormal Asylum*. He has appeared on numerous local, national and international radio programs. Clune was the cohost for the radio program *The Full Spectrum Project*, which delved into subjects including ghosts, murders and all things odd and weird, both natural and supernatural.

His other books include *California's Historic Haunts*, published by Schiffer Publishing, and the highly acclaimed *Ghosts of the* Queen Mary, published by The History Press, as well as *Ghosts and Legends of Alcatraz* and *Ghosts and Legends of Calico*, which he wrote with coauthor Bob Davis. Brian and Bob also teamed up to write the riveting biography of Ghost Box creator

Frank Sumption. Clune is also the author of *Haunted San Pedro* and *Hollywood Obscura*, the spellbinding book dealing with Hollywood's dark and sordid tales of murder and ghosts. Clune is currently working on other titles for The History Press and is teaching courses in paranormal studies at California State University, Dominguez Hills.

Brian lives in Southern California with his loving wife, Terri, his three wonderful children and, of course, Wandering Wyatt!

One of the most haunted lighthouses in the world, the Point Sur Lighthouse.

Other books by Brian Clune

Ghosts of the Queen Mary (The History Press, 2014)

California's Historic Haunts (Schiffer Publishing, 2015)

Haunted San Pedro (The History Press, 2016)

Hollywood Obscura: Death, Murder and the Paranormal Aftermath (Schiffer Publishing, 2017)

Haunted Universal Studios (The History Press, 2018)

Ghosts and Legends of Alcatraz (The History Press, 2019)

Thinking Outside the Box: Frank Sumption, Creator of the Ghost Box (Palmetto Publishing, 2019)

Ghosts and Legends of Calico (The History Press, 2020)

Haunted Heart of San Diego (The History Press, 2021)

Legends and Lore Along California's Highway 395 (The History Press, 2022)

California's Haunted Route 66 (The History Press, 2022)

Haunted Southern California (The History Press, 2022)

Dark Tourism: California (Schiffer Publishing, 2022)

Ghosts and Legends of Hollywood (The History Press, 2023)

Haunted Heart of Los Angeles (The History Press, 2024)

Brian Clune and his book *Ghosts of the* Queen Mary were featured in *The World's Most Haunted Places: Creepy, Ghostly and Notorious Spots* (*LIFE* magazine, 2016).

Visit us at
www.historypress.com